Led Zeppelin

the Complete Guide *to their* Music

OMNIBUS PRESS
London/New York
Paris/Sydney/Copenhagen
Berlin/Madrid/Tokyo

Dave Lewis

Cover and book designed by Chloë Alexander
Picture research by Sarah Bacon

ISBN: 1.84449.141.2
Order No OP49940

Exclusive Distributors
Book Sales Limited
8/9 Frith Street,
London W1D 3JB, UK.

Music Sales Corporation
257 Park Avenue South,
New York, NY 10010, USA.

Music Sales Pty Limited,
120 Rothschild Avenue, Rosebery,
NSW 2018, Australia.

To the Music Trade only:
Music Sales Limited,
8/9, Frith Street,
London W1D 3JB, UK.

Every effort has been made to trace the copyright holders
of the photographs in this book but one or two were
unreachable. We would be grateful if the photographers
concerned would contact us.

Printed by: Cox & Wyman Ltd, Reading, Berks.

A catalogue record for this book is available from the
British Library.

Visit Omnibus Press at http://www.musicsales.co.uk

Contents

INTRODUCTION

LED ZEPPELIN BEGAN LIFE AS THE VEHICLE FOR GUITARIST JIMMY PAGE TO extend the ideals of the disbanding Yardbirds, the pioneering British group whose alumni included two other outstanding guitarists, Eric Clapton and Jeff Beck. By 1968, The Yardbirds had long since passed the peak of popularity in the UK, and their hybrid style of pop psychedelia and R&B seemed to find favour only on the then emerging American FM rock radio stations and the US college and ballroom circuit.

Inspired by the chance to pursue a more adventurous and dynamic style and casting a perceptive eye on the American market, Page and manager Peter Grant set about reforming a 'new Yardbirds' line-up. Page installed seasoned musician John Paul Jones, with whom he had previously recorded in his role as a session musician, to play bass and keyboards. He initially offered the lead vocal slot to Terry Reid but he'd just signed a solo deal with producer Mickie Most and suggested Page seek out Midlands based singer Robert Plant. Plant had been working with Alexis Korner and before that carved a reputation touring with The Band Of Joy. Page and Grant checked him out and to their delight found an exciting raw talent. Plant in turn suggested hiring former Band Of Joy drummer John "Bonzo" Bonham. The new quartet played out a previously contracted Yardbirds tour of Scandinavia, renamed themselves Led Zeppelin and in October 1968 went into Olympic Studios in Barnes to cut their first album at their own expense without, as yet, a record contract.

Rarely has studio time been more economically applied. That album, simply titled *Led Zeppelin* and recorded in a mere 30 hours, set the blueprint for one of the most spectacular musical entities of the 20th century. Two decades on from their untimely demise after Bonham's death in 1980, Led Zeppelin's legacy continues to cast a giant shadow.

The reason Led Zeppelin's music has remained so durable is its sheer diversity. Though their foundations were built on blues based rock, they quickly developed a voracious musical appetite.

Page's huge, plangent riffs and John Bonham's extraordinary drumming may have dominated much of their output and unwittingly created the heavy metal genre that championed them, but as they matured Robert Plant's distinctive vocals and growing confidence as a lyricist, John Paul Jones's vast musical arranging talents, Bonham's unique drumming and Page's expanding production techniques allowed them to travel way beyond the limits of a mere rock band.

Within the Led Zeppelin catalogue you will hear strange Eastern tunings ('Kashmir'), ethereal folk arrangements ('The Battle Of Evermore'), syncopated funk rhythms ('Trampled Underfoot') and jazzy improvisations ('No Quarter'). It was that quest for experimentation that took them from soft to loud, folk to rock, blues to country and east to west.

It's a body of work that continues to inspire new generations of listeners and budding musicians. Glance any week at the Musicians Wanted/Available columns of the music mags and invariably there's a 'Guitarist seeks band – influences Led Zep' advert to be seen. Their influence is infinite.

However familiar you may be with their albums, this guide is designed to enhance the Zeppelin listening experience. It was written and researched with my own accustomed ears never too far away from the CD intray. This book now covers the band's complete catalogue from their original ten albums released between 1969 and 1982 plus the subsequent archive releases that culminated in the phenomenally successful 2003 live three-CD set and the two-disc DVD. It also logs live performances of the songs both as part of the Zeppelin era, and into the various Page, Plant and Jones live solo performances that continue to celebrate the lasting legacy of the group beyond the millennium.

Led Zeppelin's catalogue remains a vital kaleidoscope of historic rock music. This close study of their entire output will hopefully take you back to their music with a renewed perspective and a greater understanding of not only how the west was won, but how the entire world succumbed to the recorded achievements of Jimmy Page, Robert Plant, John Paul Jones and John Bonham.

Dave Lewis
December 2003

Thanks to Gary Foy, Dave Linwood, Mike Warry, Phil Tattershall, Julian Walker, Eddie Edwards, Gary Davies, Terry Boud and all the TBL crew.

DAVE LEWIS is the world renowned expert on the band and the editor and publisher of the long running Led Zeppelin magazine *Tight But Loose*. He is the author of the definitive Led Zeppelin reference books *Led Zeppelin: A Celebration* (Omnibus Press 1991) and *The Tight But Loose Files: Celebration II* (Omnibus Press 2003).

He lives in Bedford with his wife Jan and children Sam and Adam.

For details of the *Tight But Loose* magazine, e-mail
davelewis.tbl@virgin.net
or visit the *Tight But Loose* web site at
www.tblweb.com

THE TEN ALBUM LEGACY

Led Zeppelin

Atlantic Records – Original issue 588 171, re-issue K40031
UK Album Chart: No 6; US: No 10

THE DÉBUT **LED ZEPPELIN ALBUM IS THE RECORDED STATEMENT OF THEIR FIRST** few weeks together. It's also a fair representation of their initial blues/rock stage act that had been tested on Scandinavian audiences just prior to entering Olympic studios in October 1968 to lay down their first studio tracks. The material selected for the album had been well rehearsed and pre-arranged by the four, one of the primary reasons it took so little time to complete.

When it came to securing a new deal for the group, manager Peter Grant negotiated a massive five-album £200,000 package with Jerry Wexler and Ahmet Ertegun of Atlantic Records in New York. This ended speculation that they would extend The Yardbirds' previous association with Epic in America and EMI in the UK. Part of the Atlantic deal allowed Grant and Zeppelin to retain virtually complete control of artistic matters. They also formed their own company, Superhype, to handle all publishing rights. It was also agreed that all Led Zeppelin records would appear on the famous red Atlantic label, as opposed to its less distinguished Atco subsidiary which had been used for Atlantic's non-soul or R&B acts in the past. This gave them the distinction of being the first white UK act on the prestigious Atlantic label.

It took a mere 30 hours to record *Led Zeppelin* in Olympic Studios just south of the River Thames in Barnes in West London. In the hi-tech atmosphere of the Nineties, when groups of far less distinction or pedigree casually spend well over a year (and £200,000) making an album, it seems incongruous that this was all the time it took Jimmy Page and engineer Glyn Johns to produce *Led Zeppelin I*. But Led Zeppelin (or at least two of them, and manager Peter Grant) were already seasoned studio professionals and since the group didn't have a record contract at the time, Page and Grant were obliged to stump up for the studio time out of their own pockets. Unlike so many of today's profligate 'stars', there was no record company money to waste on excessive studio time; Zeppelin, acting according to an unofficial credo that in time would change the face of the record industry, were self-sufficient every step of the way.

The songs that the group recorded in a period of just nine days at a reputed cost of £1,782 had been well rehearsed and arranged on the Scandinavian tour the four undertook as The New Yardbirds, and 'old' studio hands with the experience of Page and Jones could be replied upon to get maximum value from every hour (and pound) spent at Olympic. With the possible exception of the 12 hours that The Beatles took to record their first album at Abbey Road, rarely has studio time been used so economically. Led Zeppelin's début album went on to gross more than £3.5 million, just short of 20,000 times more than they invested!

The artistic control of their output would extend to their sleeve designs and on the first album, Jimmy chose a simple black on white illustration of the Hindenburg airship going down, as Keith Moon had put it, like a 'Lead' Zeppelin. It was later claimed by The Who's John Entwistle that this sleeve design had been earmarked for the group he, Moon and Page had talked about forming a couple of years earlier. The back cover photo was taken by former Yardbird Chris Dreja, who quit to take up a career in photography during the evolution of The New Yardbirds. During the first few weeks of release in the UK, the sleeve was printed with the name and Atlantic logo in turquoise. This was switched to the common orange print later in the year, creating a much sought after sleeve rarity. The whole design was co-ordinated by George Hardie, with whom they would later work on future sleeves.

Hardie recalls that he originally offered the group a design based on an old club sign in San Francisco – a multi-sequential image of a phallic Zeppelin airship up in the clouds. Jimmy turned down the idea, but it was retained as the logo that adorned the back cover of both the first and second albums and a number of early press advertisements.

The *Led Zeppelin* album was initially released in America on January 17, 1969, to capitalise on their first US visit. Before that, Atlantic distributed a few hundred advance white label copies to key radio stations and reviewers. A positive reaction to its contents, coupled with a good reaction to their opening gigs, resulted in the album generating 50,000 advance orders. It entered the *Billboard* chart at number 99. From there it rose to number 40, then 28, reaching the Top 20 and rising as high as number 10. In all it enjoyed 73 weeks on the chart, returning for further spells in 1975 and 1979. In the UK it was issued on March 28. Originally it appeared as Atlantic 588 171 via Polydor's distribution. It was one of a new breed of stereo only releases, as up until 1969 most albums were available as stereo or mono versions. When the Warner group took over the Atlantic catalogue in 1972, the number switched to K40031. On April 12, 1969, the *Led Zeppelin* début album began a 79-week run on the British chart, peaking at number six.

The album was advertised in selected music papers under the slogan 'Led Zeppelin – the only way to fly'. And fly it certainly did. Time has done nothing to diminish the quality of one of the finest début albums ever recorded. There's an urgency and enthusiasm about their performance that retains timeless charm. The nine cuts offer a *tour de force* of powerful yet often subtle dynamics. There are just so many highlights: the spacey blues feel of 'I Can't Quit Baby', the clever light and shade approach on 'Babe I'm Gonna Leave You', Page bowing maniacally on 'Dazed And Confused' and 'How Many More Times', and throughout it all the young Robert Plant lays down a piercing vocal style set to become the group's trademark. And let's not forget the fact that with this album, Page virtually invents the guitar riff as a key songwriting component.

GOOD TIMES BAD TIMES
Page, Jones & Bonham

Studio: Olympic Studios, London

AT TWO minutes, 43 seconds, this is a perfectly compact overture to set the scene. Bonham and Jones hold down a powerful and inventive rhythm section, and when the time comes, Jimmy flexes the Telecaster (played through a Leslie speaker to create that soaring effect) in a late Yardbirds-era fashion. From the onset though, it's the Plant vocal that strikes home instantly. He executes all manner of vocal somersaults with the lyric but never loses control. Aided by a catchy chorus, 'Good Times Bad Times' is one of their most commercial offerings, and was at one time considered for release as their début single.

Live performances
Never an integral part of their set, 'Good Times Bad Times' was featured on their début tour of Scandinavia, and resurfaced on their late 1969 set as an opening

instrumental riff link for 'Communication Breakdown'. On the sixth US tour in the late summer of 1970, it returned as a vocal version inserted in the 'Communication Breakdown' medley and it made a brief return to the set during the 'Whole Lotta Love' medley played at their début show in Japan at the Budokan on September 23, 1971. Revived for one night only by Page & Plant in New Orleans on March 11 1995.

BABE I'M GONNA LEAVE YOU
Traditional – arranged by Page
(Remasters credits – Anne Bredon/Page)

Studio: Olympic

THIS WAS a number Page played to Plant from a Joan Baez album during their initial meeting at Jimmy's riverside home at Pangbourne in August 1968. It was then that he first suggested covering the song with his new-found singing partner. When it came to recording, Jimmy rearranged this traditional folk tune to fit both acoustic and electric moulds. Thus, it emerges as an early example of their musical diversity, combining the energy of a forceful Plant vocal, and a strident crash-cymbal driven chorus, with some superbly picked Spanish guitar. Vocally this track is an early flowering of Robert's much repeated 'Baby, baby, baby' vocal mannerism.

Outtake versions reveal that Plant originally approached the song with a very forceful vocal. Page, however, opted for light and shade dynamics and this required Plant to apply his softer approach on the released version as well as the more strident tones.

Though credited as a traditional arrangement, the song was actually written by an American songwriter called Anne Bredon whose own performance had been adopted by Joan Baez for her interpretation. In the early Eighties Bredon challenged Atlantic with her claim and this was accepted. There was a change of credit on the *Remasters* albums and a substantial back-payment in royalties for her.

Live performances

Used on the initial 1968/69 tours and then discarded after the second US tour. A particularly vibrant version exists from their Danish TV special filmed in March 1969. A much loved Plant song, he performed it with Fairport Convention at their Cropredy Festival in 1992 and has returned to it on his 1993 tour and with Strange Sensation in 2001/2. Revived by Page & Plant on their 1995/96 and 1998 world tours.

YOU SHOOK ME
Willie Dixon

Studio: Olympic

IT'S OFTEN forgotten just how heavily the early Led Zeppelin relied on the blues for inspiration. Their launch coincided with the British blues boom of 1968, and as can be seen from this showcase, they felt very at home in the company of standards like 'You Shook Me'. Robert in particular revelled in the song, extending the style he had perfected in The Band Of Joy to great effect. Instrumentally, the track certainly packs some punch. From Jones' swirling organ, through Plant's harmonica wailing to the point where Jimmy's solo cascades around Bonzo's stereo panned tom-tom attack, this is prime vintage Zeppelin. And the final incessant by-play between Page and Plant that leads out of the track is a masterful production technique, and one that would be further emphasised on stage.

'You Shook Me' also appeared on The Jeff Beck Group's album *Truth*. Released a few months before the début *Led Zeppelin* album, Beck has gone on record as stating that Jimmy copied their arrangement for his own devices and was well upset when the Zeppelin album stormed the charts.

Page's solo on the Zep version is

very similar to a track titled 'Jim's Blues' which he cut in his session days as a part of an album issued by the London All Stars on the French Barclay label in 1965. Plant derived the "I've got a bird that whistles" lyric from Robert Johnson's 'Stones In My Passway'.

Live performances

Featured on all the early 1968/69 tours, and then deleted for the late 1969 US tour. Revived for the US, Japan, UK and Australian dates in 1971/72, when it was part of the 'Whole Lotta Love' medley. A brief reprise of the song was tagged on to the end of 'In My Time Of Dying' at Earls Court, and on the 1977 US tour. Post Zep performed by Plant on his 1993 world tour and by Page with The Black Crowes on their US tour in 1999.

DAZED AND CONFUSED
Page

Studio: Olympic

THE ACTUAL song originates from the mid-Sixties and first appeared under the title 'I'm Confused written and sung by Jake Holmes- a New York based singer - songwriter. Jimmy took the track into The Yardbirds, re-arranged it as 'Dazed And Confused' and it was played live on stage and on radio sessions. For the début album, Page added new lyrics (somewhat surprisingly ignoring the debt the song owed to Holmes version), and spiced up the arrangement to extend the guitar played with violin bow episode. This was a technique Page was recommended during his session days by the session violinist father of actor singer David McCallum and had used onstage with The Yardbirds. The idea was also popularised by Eddie Phillips guitarist with The Creation.

The track still retains an air of menace and drama, and crystallises the electricity developing between the four at that time. It also beautifully illustrates Jones' walking bass style that lights up the track from start to finish.

Live performances

A cornerstone of every Led Zeppelin live show until 1975. It became a vehicle for intensive improvisation, often encompassing snippets of other songs. These included Plant vocal ad libs of 'Woodstock', 'Spanish Eyes', The Eagles' 'Take It Easy' and Scott Mackenzie's 'San Francisco', plus Page riffing out on 'The Crunge', 'Walter's Walk' and 'West Side Story'. It also often stretched to 30 minutes in length. On the 1975 US tour, the number had to be dropped for the first two weeks, when Jimmy injured his finger just before the tour. It made its reappearance during a stunning show at Madison Square Garden in New York on February 3. For the 1977 tour dates and Copenhagen/ Knebworth in 1979, the violin bow section was extracted from 'Dazed And Confused' to form the visual centrepiece of the set. This section was also used with The Firm and on

Page's solo Outrider tour. Performed by Plant in a rare encore version at the NEC Birmingham July 14 1993. Performed by Page & Plant as part of the Calling To You/Whole Lotta Love medleys on their 1995/96 world tour. Page also performed an instrumental version of the track at his Net Aid performance in 1999 and at his Teenage Charity concert at the Royal Albert hall in 2002.

YOUR TIME IS GONNA COME
Page, Jones

Studio: Olympic

OPENING with a grand church organ display from Jones, this track builds into a hypnotic fade-out chorus, sung by all four members. Plant's phrasing throughout is superb – 'You been bad to me woman, but it's comin' back home to you'– and Jimmy overlays some tasteful pedal steel guitar. It all evaporates beautifully into the next cut. Jones used the in house studio organ at Olympic studios and arranged the backing vocals.

Live performances
Likely to have been played on their early tour dates though no recorded evidence has emerged.Did make a one-off appearance in a medley of 'Whole Lotta Love' at the Budokan in Tokyo on September 24, 1971. Performed by Plant on a few occasions during his 1993 US tour.Performed by Page with The Black Crowes on their 1999 and 2000 US tour dates.

BLACK MOUNTAIN SIDE
Page

Studio: Olympic

THE MELODY on this Page virtuoso acoustic guitar instrumental owes more than a passing nod to an old folk song recorded by both Bert Jansch and John Renbourn, known as 'Black Waterside'. Accompanied by the tabla playing of Viram Jasani, Jimmy wades through a pleasing interlude that acts as light relief before the energy level clocks back up. Incidentally, Jimmy plays a borrowed Gibson J200 acoustic.

Page's Indian influence, also heard on 'White Summer', is on display here. During interviews for the *Remasters* albums, Page referred to CIA tuning (Celtic, Indian and Arabic) – DADGAD – which would later be employed for 'Kashmir'.

Live performances
Incorporated into the Page/Yardbirds solo number 'White Summer' on all gigs up to the fifth US jaunt in 1970. Restored to the set for the 1977 US tour, Copenhagen and Knebworth in 1979 and the 'Over Europe' tour in 1980. It later emerged in the Firm era composition 'Midnight Moonlight' and part of this number was revived by Page on his Outrider tour of 1988. Page again revived the piece on his tour of Japan with David Coverdale in 1993.

COMMUNICATION BREAKDOWN
Page, Jones, Bonham

Studio: Olympic

AN EARLY Led Zeppelin anthem, this track grew out of their Scandinavian set when it dovetailed into the show opener 'Train Kept A-Rollin'" which was played at a similar tempo. A brilliant example of Page's ability to create a whole song around a repeated guitar riff, 'Communication Breakdown' is a storming rocker that peaks just around the point Plant screams 'Suck it!' and Page cuts a screeching guitar path across the speakers. It has survived the test of time to become one of the true all time greats of the Zeppelin catalogue. It holds the distinction of being the track they performed on their one and only UK TV appearance on BBC's *How Late It Is* on March 21 1969 – and was also the very last live track they performed on their final UK appearance at Knebworth on August 11 1979.

Live performances
Developing during their first tour in September 1968, it went on to be a lasting part of their show. It was used on all dates in 1969 and in 1970 it was elevated to encore status. On the sixth US tour it was used as an encore medley. It subsequently appeared as an encore on each successive tour, including the last night at Earls Court, and the second Knebworth date. It was again an encore special for Europe 1980, and was part of Plant's 1988 and 1990 solo set. Performed by John Paul Jones with Diamanda Galas on their 1994 tour.

I CAN'T QUIT YOU BABY
Willie Dixon

Studio: Olympic

ANOTHER slow Willie Dixon blues, this is notable for its ambient production quality that brings to the fore John Bonham's wonderfully laid-back drumming, and Jimmy's deceptively mellow guitar sparring. There's a great 'just having a blow' atmosphere about this track that makes for a very relaxed outing.

Live performances
Included in their set from 1968 up to the fifth US tour in 1970. Revived as part of the 'Whole Lotta Love' medley on the Japan, UK and Europe tours 1972/3. This track was also rehearsed for the Atlantic 40th Anniversary reunion in May 1988, but was not included on the night. Page and Plant performed a version of this song at the Hammersmith show a month earlier.

They also performed it on their first reunion prior to the *Unledded* filming at the Alexis Korner benefit show staged at the Buxton Opera House on April 17 1994.

Occasionally used within 'Babe I'm Gonna Leave You' by Page & Plant on their 1995/96 shows and in 'How Many More Times' by Page & Plant on their 1998 world tour.

HOW MANY MORE TIMES
Page, Jones, Bonham

Studio: Olympic

THE CLOSING number of their early stage act and appropriately enough the parting shot of their début album, 'How Many More Times' is a lengthy, high energy exit. A marriage of Howlin Wolf's How Many More Years and The Yardbirds arrangement of Smokestack Lightning. There are also elements in the instrumental rhythm of the track Beck's Bolero cut by Page and beck in 1966. The track also owes a passing nod to a mid 60's version of 'How Many More Times' cut by Gary Farr & The T.Bones which was produced by early Yardbirds manager Giorgio Gomelsky.

From the suitably dramatic intro, complete with stinging Page wah-wah, the track develops into a medley of its own. Apparently the appearance of 'Rosie' and 'The Hunter' came spontaneously on the night of the session itself. Plant is quite fantastic here. He comes on as a supremely confident carnal gourmet boasting of much excess, but with a smile never too far from his lips. Note also Page's bowing technique. Alongside 'Dazed And Confused', this track has its origins in the old Yardbirds repertoire.

Live performances

'How Many More Times' held down the closing slot in the Zeppelin set up to and including their 1970 Bath Festival appearance. It reappeared briefly on the Japan 1971 dates, and at a date at Southampton University in January 1973. It came back into the set for the 1975 US tour, when it replaced 'Dazed And Confused' for the first two weeks due to Jimmy's injured finger. It's live appearance on the 1997 BBC Sessions album prompted Page & Plant to revive it very successfully on their 1998 world tour.

Led Zeppelin II

Atlantic Records – original issue 588198, reissue K40087
UK Album Chart: No 1; US; No 1

LITTLE TIME WAS LOST BETWEEN THE RECORDING OF THEIR DÉBUT AND THE sessions that would result in the follow-up. *Led Zeppelin II* was the group's first introduction to engineer Eddie Kramer whose work with Jimi Hendrix had already impressed Page, but studio time had to be grabbed between months of intense touring, principally in the US.

Consequently all manner of primitive studios were tried. Jimmy can recall one eight track set-up in Vancouver that didn't even boast proper headphone facilities. That the album turned out to be such a triumph, in particular for a production quality that still sounds fresh today, was in no small way due to the alliance of Page and Kramer in the control room.

One of the more successful studios Zeppelin entered for the second album was Mystic in Hollywood. Page had previously recorded there for the *Lord Sutch And Heavy Friends* album, and he returned with his new group to lay down 'The Lemon Song' completely live in Mystic's 16x16 foot room. "It had wooden walls and lots of ambience," Page recalls. "It was a small room. Richie Valens and Bobby Fuller had once recorded there, and when you listen to those Fifties records you can tell it's a small room, but the energy of it comes through."

A further recording round at Olympic and Morgan studios in London, with Kramer and assistants Andy Johns and George Chkiantz, completed the basic tracks which were then mixed over one weekend by Page and Kramer in New York. "The famous 'Whole Lotta Love' mix, where everything is going bananas, is a combination of Jimmy and myself just flying around on a small console twiddling every knob known to man," says Kramer.

In between the harder-edged material, however, there were some examples of the ever widening scope of the group's intentions. This album also marked the emergence of Robert Plant as a serious songwriter. His name had been notably absent from the début album credits due to previous contractual commitments resulting from his association with CBS Records. Now, his influence on tracks such as 'What Is And What Should Never Be' and 'Ramble On' were definite pointers to the musical future of Led Zeppelin.

Led Zeppelin II was released on October 31, 1969. In America it had advance orders for half a million copies. It entered the *Billboard* chart at 15, and by the end of the year it had dislodged The Beatles' *Abbey Road* to take the top spot, where it remained for seven weeks. By April 1970 it had registered three million American sales. It was a similar success story at home. On November 8, 1969, it began a 138-week residency on the LP chart, climbing to the top spot in February 1970.

The sleeve design was based on a David Juniper poster, and the advertising campaign was built around the slogan 'Led Zeppelin II Now Flying'. The cover illustration was based on an archive photo of the Jasta Division of the German air force with the four faces of the members of the group airbrushed on from a much used 1969 Atlantic publicity photo.

Led Zeppelin II marks a very creative period for the group, and it remains a nostalgic reflection of the sheer exuberance inspired by the intensive tour schedule aimed (successfully) at conquering America.

WHOLE LOTTA LOVE
Page, Bonham, Plant, Jones

Studios: Olympic; Sunset Sound, Los Angeles; A and R, New York

THE CATALYST. A masterful Page/Kramer production. From Plant's off-mike cough through to the 'Keepa coolin' baby' squeals, this is five minutes and 33 seconds of aural and sexual delight. The song originally took shape around Page's killer three-note riff with its octave E conclusion, and a descending chord structure which employed backwards echo effects first used by Jimmy on a Mickie Most session. Devoid of their own lyrics, Plant took some from Willie Dixon's 'You Need Love'. In failing to credit Dixon, the group were subsequently sued and they settled out of court.

But the most impressive part of 'Whole Lotta Love' had nothing whatsoever to do with Willie Dixon. This was the apocalyptic central section in which Page mixed all manner of crazy sound effects – full tilt whoops, screams, sirens and demolition noises interspersed with what sounded remarkably like Robert squealing in orgasmic bliss from the depths of a coal mine – into a truly mind-blowing sequence which careered wildly from speaker to speaker and suggested total mayhem.

This section was missing – inevitably – when 'Whole Lotta Love' was edited down to become a Top Five hit single in America. It also reached number one in Belgium and Germany. In the UK, Atlantic had expected to issue the edited version themselves, and pressed initial copies for release on December 5, 1969. However, Peter Grant halted the release, stating that to issue singles off albums was not Led Zeppelin's policy. An official statement added that they had written a special number which they intended to be their first British single. This never materialised, and despite much record company pressure, they declined to issue official singles in the UK throughout their career. 'Whole Lotta Love' was eventually released as a single in the UK in September 1997 to support the re issue of the Zep catalogue.

In many respects 'Whole Lotta Love' would become a millstone around Led Zeppelin's collective neck. An instrumental version of the song by CCS (aka Collective Consciousness Society), a large studio group put together by Alexis Korner and Danish bluesman Peter Thorup, became the signature tune for the UK weekly TV chart show *Top Of The Pops*, thus ensuring that it would seep into the consciousness of every pop fan in the land, whether or not they were fans of Led Zeppelin.

It also came to be regarded – quite rightly – as the definitive expression of heavy metal, a term of reference yet to come into common usage when *Led Zeppelin II* was released, and as a result Led Zeppelin would eventually become known as the definitive heavy metal band. It was a pejorative description they would come to abhor, which they would never be able to shake off, and which they certainly didn't deserve. They were not to know how many thousands of future bands would rip off the concept of 'Whole Lotta Love' – the directness of a repeated riff awash in echo – in the years to come or how many bands would take their style and look, simplify it for easy access, mass consumption and sheer escapism, and refer to it and themselves as heavy metal. Musical eclecticism was Led Zeppelin's real hallmark, and that eclecticism incorporated much more than the simple yet explosive noise that was 'Whole Lotta Love'.

Live performances

'Whole Lotta Love' made its live début on the second US tour in April 1969 as part of a medley with 'As Long As I Have You'. In June 1969 they previewed it on a BBC session. It was then part of each subsequent set list. For the early 1970 dates it was an encore number. From the sixth US tour in 1970 up to the 1973 US tour, it was the closing finale of every Zeppelin performance, extending in length to include a rock'n'roll medley. On their 1975 dates it was an encore medley with 'Black Dog' and in 1977 it was used as a medley encore with 'Rock And Roll' and, on one occasion at the LA Forum, with 'Communication Breakdown'. It was given a new arrangement for the 1979 Copenhagen/Knebworth encores (the same version was revived for the Atlantic 40th Anniversary reunion in May 1988), and returned to the 'Let That Boy Boogie' medley workout for the 1980 Europe dates. It holds the distinction of being the last track Led Zeppelin performed live, when it received a 17-minute work-out at the final gig in Berlin on July 7, 1980. It was also played at the Live Aid get-together on July 13, 1985. Post Zep :performed by Plant on his 1993 and 2000/2002 tours. Revived by Page & Plant for their 1995/96 and 1998 world tours. Performed by Page with David Coverdale on a show in Nagoya on their 1993 Japanese tour and with The Black Crowes on their 1999/2000 US tour dates.

WHAT IS AND WHAT SHOULD NEVER BE
Page, Plant

Studios: Olympic; Groove, New York; A and R

THE GENESIS of Robert Plant's career as a songwriter, this dreamy affair is a departure from the dizzy atmosphere of 'Whole Lotta Love'. It's also another superb Page production with its flanging vocal effects and powerful stereo separation on the fade out. Jimmy had switched to the Gibson Les Paul for recording, and the sustained solo here is quite beautiful. The song gained more attention when Plant revived it on his 1993 Fate Of Nations tour and subsequently when played live by Page & Plant on their world tours. Page also selected it as the radio airplay cut from his *Excess All Areas-Live At The Greek* album drawn from appearances with The Black Crowes in 1999.

Live performances
Previewed in June 1969 on a BBC radio session, premièred at the London Lyceum on October 12 and then inserted on the late 1969 US tour and played at every gig through 1970/71 up to the US tour in June 1972. Discarded thereafter. Performed by Plant on his 1993 world tour. Revived by Page & Plant at their MTV *Unledded* London filming in 1994 and on their 1995/96 and 1998 world tours. Performed by Page with The Black Crowes on their 1999 and 2000 US tour dates.

THE LEMON SONG
Chester Burnett

Studios: Mystic, Los Angeles; A and R

THIS TRACK was originally credited to Page, Plant, Jones and Bonham but claims from publishers Jewel Music that the song was heavily based on Chester (Howlin' Wolf) Burnett's 'Killing Floor' led to another settlement and a change of sleeve credit. In fact some later copies of the album do list the track as 'Killing Floor'. This arrangement also takes from Albert King's 'Cross-Cut Saw', a staple of the gigs Plant would perform with The Honeydrippers in 1981. Recorded virtually live in New York's Mystic studios, the track combined 'Killing Floor', which they had been performing at their early gigs, with the Robert Johnson inspired 'squeeze my lemon' sequence with its intense erotic overtones.

Live performances
'Killing Floor' was used on the début American tour, and was to evolve into 'The Lemon Song' for the second and third tours. Dropped in late 1969, though the 'squeeze my lemon' sequence was often inserted into the 'Whole Lotta Love' medley and ad-libbed elsewhere. Lines from the song were also occasionally used within 'How Many More Times' on Page & Plant's 1998 world tour. Revived by Page in the 'Zep 2' arrangement for his 1999/2000 dates with The Black Crowes.

THANK YOU
Page, Plant

Studios: Morgan, London; A and R

THIS EMOTIONAL love song to his wife brings out the best in Robert Plant, as he commits to tape one of his finest vocal performances. Elsewhere in the arrangement John Paul Jones excels on Hammond organ, and Jimmy complements it all with some delicate Rickenbacker 12-string picking. A long standing favourite of the composers, it was the number Page and Plant selected to open their 1994 historic MTV *Unledded* filming sessions at the London Studios on August 25 1994.

Live performances
Made its début in the set on the January 1970 UK tour. Stayed in the show throughout 1970/71 acting as a spotlight for Jones' keyboard solo. Used as a marathon encore on the 1972/3 tours and then deleted from the act. At the Freddie Mercury Tribute Concert at Wembley Stadium in April 1992, Plant sang a few lines from the song as a bridge intro to his version of Queen's 'Crazy Little Thing Called Love'. Performed by Plant on his 1993 tour. Revived by Page & Plant at the MTV *Unledded* London filming in 1994 and on their 1995/6 and 1998 world tours.

HEARTBREAKER
Page, Plant, Jones, Bonham

Studio: A and R

HEARTBREAKER' is another integral part of the recorded Zeppelin canon and a perfect platform for Page to display his guitar virtuosity. On this studio cut, he offers up a breathtaking exercise in string-bending guitar technique, while on the road he extended the track to include snippets of Bach's Lute Suite No 1 and Simon & Garfunkel's '59th Street Bridge Song'. One of the great all time Zeppelin riffs as acknowledged in the 90's by the US TV cartoon *Beavis And Butthead*.

Live performances
A long-standing live favourite, it joined the set at the Lyceum in October 1969. From the Bath Festival onwards and throughout the rest of their dates in 1970/71, it provided a dual thrust set opener with 'Immigrant Song'. For the US, Japan, UK and Europe tours of 1972/73, it became part of the encore. It was back in the main set as a medley with 'Whole Lotta Love' for the 1973 US dates (see *The Song Remains The Same* movie), and then an encore again on the 1975 US tour, the last night at Earls Court, selected dates during 1994 the 1977 US tour, Knebworth 1, and the Europe 1980 tour. It was also performed at the Atlantic 40th Anniversary reunion in 1988.

Additional colouring that Page brought to this track included a few chords from 'Greensleeves' and a regular instrumental passage based on Bach's 'Bourée' in C minor. When employed as an encore during the 1975 US tour, versions of 'That's Alright' and 'I'm A Man' were inserted into the song at Madison Square Garden (Feb 12) and Long Beach (March 12) respectively. Revived by Page & Plant on their 1995/96 and 1998 world tours. Performed by Page with The Black Crowes on their 1999 and 2000 US tour dates. A snippet of the song was deployed by John Paul Jones within his solo track Bass'N'Drums on his 1999 tour dates.

LIVIN' LOVIN' MAID (SHE'S JUST A WOMAN)
Page, Plant

Studios: Morgan, London; A and R, New York

JIMMY returned to the Telecaster to knock out what the band always considered to be something of a production line filler. However, this tight, hook-laden ditty, found much favour on the radio, and when 'Whole Lotta Love' finished its chart run in America, 'Livin' Lovin' Maid' was flipped over to become an A-side in its own right. It then climbed to Number 65 on the *Billboard* chart. The song is rumoured to be about one of their early, persistent West Coast groupies.

Live performances
Such was their distaste for this track, it never received a full public

airing. On a date in Hamburg in March 1970 Plant slipped the first line of the song into 'Heartbreaker' and he sang the opening line in jest at Earls Court on May 24, 1975. Explaining the intention of this show he said, "We don't just mean we're gonna groove around on anything that could be groovy like 'With the purple umbrella and the 50 cent hat' no... none of that!" In a surprise move Plant brought the song into his 'Manic Nirvana' US/UK solo tour set in 1990, turning it into a rousing encore with a Beach Boys style.

RAMBLE ON
Page, Plant

Studios: Juggy Sound; A and R

ENTER THE ethereal Page and Plant. 'Ramble On', with its Tolkien-inspired lyrical content was for Plant in particular the highlight of *Led Zeppelin II*. It remains a splendid illustration of the light and shade dynamism that would characterise so much of their future work. It slips effortlessly from quiet mournful passages into an uplifting chorus, and Page's overdubbed interweaving Gibson run is an early attempt at the guitar army assault that would become his trademark. A long standing favourite still performed with gusto by Plant on his 2002 tour with Strange Sensation.

Live performances
Surprisingly, 'Ramble On' was never performed live in a full version. On the Spring 1970 US tour Plant did

throw in lines from the song during 'Communication Breakdown' (see 'Mudslide' bootleg) and 'Whole Lotta Love'. Performed by Plant on his 1993/2002 tours and a much performed song on Page & Plant's 1995/6 and 1998 world tours.

MOBY DICK
Bonham, Jones, Page

Studios: Mirror Sound, L.A.; May Fair, New York; A and R

JOHN Bonham's percussive showcase took shape on the second US tour when it was known as 'Pat's Delight' (a reference to his wife). Built between a killer Page riff, used as the theme to BBC 2's *Disco 2* rock show, Bonzo does his thing with sticks and bare hands.

Outtakes from the Zeppelin II sessions reveal the 'Moby Dick' drum solo to have been edited down from a much longer version. The riff part of the track can be traced back to the BBC unused session track 'The Girl I Love' which was laid down in the summer of 1969.

Live performances
Came in on the 1969 November US tour and stayed in the set on every tour up to 1977 although it was not played at every single show. It developed into an excessive 20-minute showcase which provided the others with a break in the show. By 1975 Bonzo was incorporating a 'Whole Lotta Love' riff segment played on electronically treated kettle drums. On the 1977 US tour, the track was aptly renamed 'Over The Top', and employed the riff of 'Out On The Tiles' instead of the 'Moby Dick' theme.

BRING IT ON HOME
Page, Plant

Studios: Mystic, Los Angeles; Atlantic New York; A and R

OPENS WITH a straight lift from Sonny Boy Williamson's 'Bring It On Home' with Plant on harmonica. It soon snaps into electric action via a rivetting Page riff and Bonham beef up.

Live performances
Used on stage from the November 1969 US tour and retained for their 1970 itinerary. Live, it developed into a lengthy piece with a great Page/Bonham guitar-drum battle. Revived briefly for the 1972 US tour as an encore (as can be heard on the 'How The West Was Won' live CD) and re-employed on the 1973 US tour as an opening sequence riff link to merge 'Celebration Days' with 'Black Dog', 'Bring It On Home' was also played at the reunion staged at Jason Bonham's wedding reception in May 1990. Revived by Page & Plant on their 1995/96 and 1998 world tours. Performed by Page with the Black Crowes on their 1999 and 2000 US tour dates.

Led Zeppelin III

Atlantic – original issue 2401002, reissued as K50002
UK Album Chart: No 1; US: No 1

After the often absurd studio conditions enduring for the second album, the group made a conscious effort to alter the pace of future recording. Fortunately their strategy for self-sufficiency had paid off in spades, and it was most unlikely that there would ever be a repeat of the pressures that caused them to record as hurriedly as they had in 1969. Fate, as we shall see, would change all that down the line but in the meantime their third album could be approached at a considerably more leisurely pace.

Page and Plant set the ball rolling with their much documented trip to Bron-Y-Aur, a remote cottage on the side of Snowdonia where they could play and compose into the night, working by candlelight and the soft glow of a wood fire. Such surroundings – and the lack of electric power – not unnaturally signalled a slight change of direction with an emphasis on acoustic arrangements.

After preparing the material that would emerge on *Led Zeppelin III*, they rehearsed the songs at a run-down mansion in Hampshire. This proved to be a significant move. With its relaxed atmosphere and rural surroundings, Headley Grange provided a favoured alternative to the discipline of a conventional studio.

The third album was recorded in a series of May/June sessions at Headley Grange and Olympic with Andy Johns engineering. Some additional work was put in at the newly opened Island Studios in London's Notting Hill in July. It was all wrapped up with a mixdown at Ardent Studios in Memphis during Zeppelin's sixth American tour in August 1970.

The whole album proved to be a watershed release, not only in content and construction, but also in composition. After Page's domination of the first two albums, the third was a more democratic affair, and given increased rehearsal time, all four group members were able to offer up their own compositions and ideas. It was a pattern that would continue in future sessions.

Led Zeppelin III was the most eagerly awaited album of 1970. After what was to become a traditional Led Zeppelin delay (this time two months), it finally surfaced in October of that year. Advance orders in America were close to the million mark, and it spent four weeks at the top of the *Billboard* chart. It entered the British chart at number one and remained there for three weeks. It returned to the top for a further week on December 12.

The elaborate gatefold sleeve, which held up release, was designed by

Richard Drew, a lecturer in fine arts at Leeds Polytechnic. Its rotating inner wheel, an idea of Page's, was based on crop rotation charts but the end result was not quite how Jimmy had originally conceived it. Its release was trailered by a full page ad taken out in the *Melody Maker* at the end of September. In a reference to their runaway success in that year's *Melody Maker* readers' poll, the ad simply said, "Thank you for making us the world's number one band".

The diverse content of the album, with its accent on more acoustically based arrangements, confused both critics and the public alike. Hindsight was to prove that this change in direction was a natural progression for the group. At no point would they restrict themselves to one musical genre.

Led Zeppelin III is another triumph for Jimmy Page as a producer. He brings out the best qualities of each song here, from the dramatic intro of 'Since I've Been Loving You' through to the delicacy of 'That's The Way'. It all adds up to one of their most absorbing and intimate listening experiences.

IMMIGRANT SONG
Page, Plant

Studios: Headley Grange, Hampshire; Island and Olympic, London; Ardent, Memphis

NOTHING less than a classic. Built around an incessant Page/Jones/Bonham battering riff, this Plant tale of Viking lust is a compulsive attack on the senses as well as a call to arms. In addition to containing some of Plant's most memorable lines, it also boasts a wailing war-cry destined to delight rabid audiences across the world.

The basis of this track was already recorded before their trip to play in Iceland on June 22, 1970. It was this vacation that inspired Robert to construct a new set of lyrics full of Icelandic imagery. As he put it in a 1970 radio interview: "We went to Iceland, and it made you think of Vikings and big ships... and John Bonham's stomach... and bang, there it was – 'Immigrant Song'!"

The count in at the start, by the way, is coupled with echo tape feedback – hence the hiss. In America 'Immigrant Song' was lifted as a single and after a 13-week chart run peaked at 16.

The visual and aural combination of this track as sourced from the 1972 Long Beach show and Sydney Showground cine film and used on the 2003 Led Zeppelin DVD is a stark reminder of the sheer power of this composition.

Live performances

'Immigrant Song' was premièred to UK audiences at the opening of Led Zeppelin's 1970 Bath Festival appearance. This version features varying verses to the later studio issue. The live arrangement included an extended guitar solo. It was the set opener of every show played from Bath 1970 up to the 1972 US tour. For the Japan, UK and Europe 1972/73 dates it emerged as part of the encore. It was then deleted from the set. One odd live improvisation occurred on August 22, 1971, at the LA Forum when 'Immigrant Song' opened the set and Page prefaced the intro with a few bars of The Ventures' 'Walk Don't Run'. Robert Plant was to revive the song in an amended arrangement on his solo tours of 1988/1990. Also used as a riff intro to 'Wanton Song' by Page & Plant on their 1995/96 world tour.

FRIENDS
Page, Plant

Studios: Olympic; Ardent

A FEW SECONDS of studio chat precedes this hypnotic swirling mass of sound. It's surprising that John Paul Jones has no composing credit here, as he is wholly responsible for the track's compelling string arrangement. There's a Moog synthesiser added on the outro which provides a link to the next track. With its repeated acoustic guitar motifs and bongo percussion, this bizarre outing was unlike anything else they attempted.

Page used an Altair Tube Limiter to enhance the acoustic quality of his Harmony guitar, a device recommended by Dick Rosemenie, an acoustic guitarist who recorded an album entitled 'Six String, Twelve String and Vanguard'. The same device was used on 'All My Love' on the 'In Through The Out Door' album.

'Friends' employs another odd tuning. Jimmy: "Top E is E, B is a C, G is a G, D is a C, A remains the same, and the low E goes down to C. We also did that on 'Bron-Y-Aur' and 'Poor Tom'."

Live performances
The only documented live performance of 'Friends' is a version played in Osaka on the 1971 Japanese tour. This was also, along with 'Four Sticks', one of the experimental songs Jimmy and Robert recorded with the Bombay Orchestra in March 1972. It was however extensively performed by Page & Plant on their 1995/6 world tour and performed at the MTV *Unledded* London filming in 1994.

CELEBRATION DAY
Page, Plant, Jones

Studios: Headley Grange; Island; Olympic; Ardent

A TRACK that nearly didn't appear at all. Due to a studio oversight, the intro of this track was crinkled on the master tape, making it impossible to thread, but by segueing the swirling link from 'Friends' into the guitar riff and Plant's opening lyrics, the song was salvaged. A good thing too, as it's an excellent vehicle for a succession of Page's guitar effects, and Plant's happy tour of New York.

Live performances

Came in to the set as part of a medley with 'Communication Breakdown' at the KB Hallen date in Copenhagen in the spring of 1971, then used on the late summer tour of America in 1971, and stayed for the Japanese, UK and Australian tours of late 1971 early 1972. Revived for the 1973 US dates and then again for the Copenhagen and Knebworth gigs in 1979. Revived by Page & Plant for their 1995/6 and 1998 world tours. Performed by Page with The Black Crowes on their 1999 and 2000 US tour dates. Performed by Plant with Strange Sensation on his 2002 tour.

SINCE I'VE BEEN LOVING YOU
Page, Plant

Studios: Island; Olympic; Ardent

ONE OF the first songs prepared for Led Zeppelin III, it was previewed as early as the January tour of the UK in 1970. A self-styled and somewhat mannered slow blues, with some lovely organ from J.P., it featured one of Jimmy's most expressive solos prefaced by a dramatic shout of 'Watch out!' from Plant.

Live performances

Entered the set in early 1970 and retained throughout their 1970/71 dates. From the Japan tour in 1972 up to the 1973 American dates, it formed the second half of a medley

with 'Misty Mountain Hop'. It came back into the set in its own right for the latter part of the 1975 US tour, and reappeared for the 1977 US tour, Copenhagen/Knebworth 1979, and Europe 1980. On Plant's solo tours part of the track was aired in 'Slow Dancer'. Also performed in a version at Hammersmith in 1988 with Page guesting. Revived by Page & Plant at their MTV *Unledded* London filming in 1994 and their 1995/96 world tour.

OUT ON THE TILES
Page, Plant, Bonham

Studios: Headley Grange; Olympic; Ardent, Memphis

AFTER PAGE'S domination of the first two albums, the more leisurely paced recording of *Led Zeppelin III* allowed for a more democratic pool of ideas. This track came out of a Bonham-inspired riff and is a much underrated part of their output. With an infectious chorus and enthusiastic Plant vocal, it bubbles along with an unnerving energy. The title relates to a previously written set of lyrics that were revamped for this version. The spacey sound mix evident here is another example of distance miking in the studio by Page.

Live performances

This track was only ever used on the sixth US tour of September 1970. However, the opening riff was later applied to the live arrangement of 'Black Dog'. Then on the 1977 US tour the riff structure of 'Out On The Tiles' replaced 'Moby Dick' as the lead intro to Bonham's drum solo which was retitled by Plant as 'Over The Top'. The riff was also used to open Black Dog on Page & Plant's 1995/96 and 1998 world tours. Performed by Page with the Black crowes on their 1999 and 2000 US tour dates.

GALLOWS POLE
Traditional: arranged by Page and Plant

Studios: Headley Grange; Olympic; Ardent

THIS traditional folk tune can be traced back to Leadbelly. His version titled 'Gallis Pole' can be found on *The Leadbelly Story* (DVRECD 39). Another version is on an album by Odetta, *The Leadbelly Essential Odetta* (Vanguard VCD 43/44). Other blues variations of the tune of the song have been recorded as 'Gallows Line' and 'Maid Freed From the Gallows'. Jimmy adapted it from a version by Fred Gerlach.

Instrumentally, it has Page on banjo, six and 12-string acoustic guitar and electric guitar. John Paul Jones is on mandolin and bass. While Plant unfolds a tale of medieval woe, the tension builds beautifully as Bonzo wades in, and Page adds an understated but frenzied Gibson run. One of their most adventurous outings and quite brilliant in its execution – lyrically and musically.

Live performances
Played on some of the March/May/June UK and European tour dates in 1971. Robert did sometimes throw in some lines of this during 'Trampled Underfoot', remarking on its performance on the last night of the 1975 US tour in LA as being 'Trampled Under Gallows'. Performed by Plant on his 2003 tour with strange Sensation. Revived by Page & Plant at their MTV *Unledded* London filming in 1994 and on their 1995/6 and 1998 world tours.

TANGERINE
Page

Studios: Headley Grange; Olympic; Ardent

JIMMY provides an eight-second count-in to a mellow solo composition left over from his Yardbirds era. Robert duets with himself on a double-tracked vocal, and Pagey layers on some tasteful pedal steel guitar.

Live performances
Joined the acoustic set on the Japanese dates in September 1971. Remained in the set on all tours up to the US dates in the summer of 1972. Revived as a four-part harmony rendition for the Earls Court season in 1975, for which Jimmy pulled out the Gibson double-neck. Further revived by Page & Plant on their 1995/6 and 1998 world tours.

THAT'S THE WAY
Page, Plant

Studios: Headley Grange; Olympic; Ardent

ONE OF their very best performances and definitely Robert's best ever lyric, 'That's The Way' carried the working title of 'The Boy Next Door'. Written at the cottage in Bron-Y-Aur, it centres around the dissolution of a pair of star crossed lovers. The lyrics were influenced in part by the unrest Robert witnessed on their Spring 1970 US travels. The tale unfolds against a rush of acoustic guitars, and a moving horn-like electric solo from Jimmy.

Live performances
Premièred at Bath, and a standard feature of the acoustic set during 1970/71 and up to the American tour in 1972. Recalled for the Earls Court season in 1975. Revived by Page & Plant at their MTV *Unledded* London filming and on their 1995/96 world tour. Performed and sung by John Paul Jones on his 2001 tour dates.

BRON-Y-AUR STOMP
Page, Plant, Jones

Studios: Headley Grange; Olympic; Ardent

SOME LIGHT relief. A playful folksy singalong, written at the cottage about Plant's dog Strider. Page gets in some fine picking, Bonzo adds spoons and castanets, and Jones plays an acoustic bass. The tune itself was tried in an electric rockier arrangement at the commencement of the third album sessions late in 1969, when it was known as 'Jennings Farm Blues'.

Live performances
Used in the acoustic set from the UK dates in Spring 1971 through to the American tour in 1972. A revamped arrangement with Jones on stand-up bass was used for the Japan/UK/Europe 1972/73 dates. Recalled in this format for Earls Court in 1975, and then as a medley with 'Black Country Woman' on the 1977 US tour.

HATS OFF TO (ROY) HARPER
Traditional; arranged by Charles Obscure

Studios: Headley Grange; Olympic; Ardent

A PAGE/PLANT jam, loosely based on Bukka White's old blues tune 'Shake 'Em On Down'. Page gets in some authentic bottleneck guitar. The title is an acknowledgement of their admiration for the eccentric Mr Harper. Page and Plant first met him at the Bath festival in 1970 and became long standing admirers. Page would later record an album *Whatever Happened To Jugula* with Harper issued in 1985. A six-minute, blues medley was also recorded during this session.

Live performances
None.

Atlantic Records – original issue 2401 OZ 2, reissued as K 50008
UK Album Chart: No 1: US: No 2

WHEN **L**ED **Z**EPPELIN **RETURNED TO** **H**EADLEY **G**RANGE **IN EARLY 1971,** **THEY** took along The Rolling Stones' mobile studio to record the whole process. "We needed the sort of facilities where we could have a cup of tea and wander around the garden and then go in and do what we had to do," said Page. By moving into Headley Grange for the whole period of recording, many of the tracks were made up almost on the spot and committed to tape almost there and then.

"A recording studio is an immediate imposition as compared to sitting around a fire strumming," said Robert Plant at the time. "With Headley Grange we can put something down and hear the results immediately."

Initial sessions for the fourth album began at the new Island studios in December 1970, but the real work was done in the country. Once inside the great hall of Headley Grange, ideas flowed freely. It was here that Page stumbled on that monster snare and bass drum sound by spaciously miking Bonzo's newly acquired kit.

With the basic tracks recorded, many of them live, they added overdubs at Island and on the recommendation of engineer Andy Johns took the completed master tapes to Los Angeles Sunset Sound Studios for mixing. This mix proved to be a great disappointment, causing a delay in the release of the album. They had hoped to have it out in time for their late summer tour of the US, but further mixing back in London put the release back to November.

After the mixed reception that greeted *Led Zeppelin III*, the group deliberately played down the release of their fourth album. There had been talk of releasing a double set at one time, and at one stage Jimmy came up with the idea of issuing the fourth album as four EPs.

When it came to a title, instead of the expected *Led Zeppelin IV*, they decided to set a precedent by selecting four symbols, each representing a member of the band, to form the title. Each member chose his own symbol. John Bonham's came from a book of runes and took the form of three linked circles. Said to represent the man-wife-child trilogy, Plant was heard to remark that it resembled the emblem of Ballantine beer! John Paul Jones' came from the same book and is meant to represent confidence and competence. Plant's feather in a circle design was his own, based on the sign of the ancient Mu civilisation. Jimmy Page's mysterious symbol, which has often been mistaken for a word that could be pronounced 'Zoso', was also his own work. The group could hardly have known at the time what lasting imagery these symbols would have on their following.

To further throw the media (and the music industry, their fans and everyone else), the gatefold sleeve design was entirely wordless except for a barely decipherable Oxfam poster hanging amidst the urban decay depicted on the front. This cover print was actually bought from a junk shop in Reading by Plant. A tarot card illustration of the Hermit formed the inner gatefold illustration and the lyrics to 'Stairway To Heaven' were printed on the inner sleeve. Atlantic Records' reaction to this total lack of information on the sleeve was predictably negative.

As a result of all this mystery, no-one has ever been quite sure what to actually call the album, and it has been variously referred to over the years as *Led Zeppelin IV*, *Untitled*, *Four Symbols*, *Zoso* and *The Runes*. And since no-one from the Zeppelin camp has ever actually confirmed a title, the mystery is unlikely ever to be solved – which is exactly what the increasingly mysterious Led Zeppelin wanted.

In the run up to the album's release a series of teaser adverts depicting each symbol was placed in the music press. It did not take their fans too long to associate these mystical images with the album, and, title or no title, the fourth Zeppelin album was an instant massive seller. It entered the UK chart at number one and stayed on the chart for 62 weeks. In America it remained on the chart longer than any other Zeppelin album, though it failed to knock Carole King's mega-selling *Tapestry* off the top. Ultimately the fourth Zeppelin album would be the most durable seller in their catalogue and the most impressive critical and commercial success of their career.

In December 1990, this album, along with Def Leppard's *Hysteria*, was certified by *Billboard* magazine as being the biggest selling rock album in American chart history. By that year's end it had registered some 10 million sales in the US alone. Not bad for an album whose wordless sleeve artwork was declared commercial suicide when it was first handed to the record company.

BLACK DOG
Page, Plant, Jones

Studios: Headley Grange, Hampshire, with The Rolling Stones' Mobile; Island, London

IF *ZEPPELIN III* had thrown up doubts in some corners as to their ability to still flex the power dis-played on the first two albums, here was the perfect antidote. The moment Page warms up the Gibsons, this is one of the most instantly recognisable Zepp tracks.

The impossible part of the riff was a Jones input, while the *a cappella* vocal arrangement, Page would admit years later, was influenced by Fleetwood Mac's 'Oh Well'.

The solo is constructed out of four overdubbed Les Paul fills. 'Black Dog' takes its title from a mutt that hung around at the Grange. It is held in great esteem by Plant in particular, who would later add snippets of the song into his solo tracks 'Tall Cool One', and 'Your Ma Said She Cried In Her Sleep Last Night'.

*** ***

Live performances

Joined the set on the UK tour at Belfast's Ulster Hall on March 5, 1971. Retained for each subsequent tour up to the 1973 US tour. Used as an encore medley with 'Whole Lotta Love' on the 1975 US tour and Earls Court. Hardly used in 1977 (the July 23 Oakland show saw its appearance as a rare second encore). Recalled to the set for the 1979 Copenhagen/Knebworth dates and Europe 1980 (complete with rare spoken intro from Jimmy). Revived by Page & Plant on their 1995/96 and 1998 world tours. Performed by Page with David Coverdale on their Japanese tour in 1993. Performed in an instrumental version by John Paul Jones on his 1999/2001 tour.

ROCK AND ROLL
Page, Plant, Jones, Bonham

Studios: Headley Grange, with The Rolling Stones' Mobile; Island

A NOTHER instantly identifiable Zeppelin anthem. This track came out of a jam with Rolling Stones' mentor Ian Stewart on piano. Bonzo played the intro of 'Good Golly Miss Molly'/'Keep A Knockin", and Page added a riff. Fifteen minutes later the nucleus of 'Rock And Roll' was down on tape – displaying the full benefit of recording on location with the tapes ever running.

Live performances

A lasting part of their history, 'Rock And Roll' came in as an encore on the spring 1971 dates when it was referred to by Plant as 'It's Been A Long Time'. It was inserted into the main set for the US, Japanese, UK and Australian tour schedule of 1971/2. When they revamped the set in late 1972 for the Japan and UK dates it was elevated to the opening number, probably because its first line – "It's been a long time since I rock and rolled" – was highly appropriate for a show opener. It retained this status on every show up to the Earls Court season in 1975. It became a medley encore with 'Whole Lotta Love' in America in 1977. For Knebworth and Europe it was an encore in its own right. Post-Zeppelin, it has enjoyed airings at Live Aid, at Hammersmith with Plant and Page in 1988, at Jason Bonham's wedding bash, and The Knebworth Silver Clef reunion. Performed by Page with David Coverdale on their Japanese tour in 1993. Performed by Plant on his 1993/4 world tour. Revived by Page & Plant on their 1995/6 and 1998 world tours.

THE BATTLE OF EVERMORE
Page, Plant

Studios: Headley Grange with The Rolling Stones' Mobile; Olympic, London

THE TUNE for this was written by Page late one night at the Grange while he experimented on Jones' mandolin. Robert came up with a set of lyrics inspired by a book he was reading on the Scottish wars. Sandy Denny was called in to sing the answer lines to Plant's play-ette. Another impressive arrangement. A solo Plant guide vocal out-take remains in the vaults.

This song appeared in the 1992 grunge cult film *Singles*, performed by The Love Mongers who featured Annie and Nancy Wilson of Heart.

Live performances

Only ever played live by Zeppelin on the 1977 US tour, with John Paul Jones taking on the dual vocal task. Revived by Page & Plant at their MTV *Unledded* London filming in 1994 in an ambitious arrangement with Najma Akhtar on vocals and on their 1995/6 world tour.

STAIRWAY TO HEAVEN
Page, Plant

Studios: Headley Grange with The Rolling Stones' Mobile; Island

THE BIG ONE. 'Stairway' started out as a fairly complete chord progression that Page brought in when they commenced recording at

Island studios in December 1970. At Headley Grange the song developed around the log fire with Robert composing a set of lyrics full of hippy mysticism that told the tale of a search for spiritual perfection. The song's arrangement with Jones contributing bass recorder on the intro and Bonzo entering as the track built to a crescendo, came together very quickly. This left Jimmy to add the solo, for which he returned to the Telecaster, back at Island. For the live version he would invest in a custom-made Gibson SG double-neck guitar.

'Stairway To Heaven' was undoubtedly the stand out track on the fourth album, and was well received when they performed it on the UK and US dates prior to the album's release. When they went back to the States in the summer of 1972, Atlantic were naturally keen to issue the track as a single. Grant refused and was to do the same again the next year. The upshot of that decision was that record buyers began to invest in the fourth album as if it were a single.

'Stairway To Heaven' went on to become the most requested song on American radio, and achieve truly classic status worldwide. Far from being a mere rock song, it has become something of a people's favourite, cover version fodder for symphony orchestras and night club singers alike. So well known has the dreamy opening riff become that guitarists trying out guitars in music shops must pay a fine of £5 if they play 'Stairway' in the shop! In 1993 an entire album of cover versions of 'Stairway To Heaven' by various Australian performers instigated by the Australian *Money Or The Gun* TV show was released, and a spoof rendering by the inimitable Rolf Harris found its way into the UK Top Ten amid much jocularity.

Alongside songs like 'A Whiter Shade Of Pale' and 'You've Lost That Loving Feeling', 'Stairway' has a pastoral opening cadence that is classical in feel and which has ensured its immortality. This air of respectability may be the reason why Robert Plant has turned away from the song, declaring it a great song written at the right time for all the right reasons, but now sanctimonious in the extreme. Free from the burden of having to interpret the lyrics, Jimmy Page remains justly proud of the composition, happy to celebrate its legacy as an instrumental live showpiece.

On the 20th anniversary of the original release of this song, it was announced via US radio sources that the song had logged up an estimated 2,874,000 radio plays – back to back that would run for 44 years solid. Its reverence in America remains unparalleled. In the UK there was a strong lobby from both Warners and Radio One to see the track issued as a single for the Christmas market in 1990. Ultimately – and unsurprisingly – the idea was vetoed. Rare original seven inch promos pressed at the time, accompanied by a humourous in-house memo (Atlantic LZ3), are amongst the most sought after UK rarities.

When they sat around that log fire all those years ago, they certainly could never have envisaged the impact 'Stairway To Heaven' would have on their career, that the song would become the single most requested track on American FM radio for most of the Seventies, or that it would inspire a whole album of cover versions.

The appearance of the superb delivery of the song drawn from their Earl's Court shows in May 1975 on the 2003 Led Zeppelin DVD finally restored some much overdue dignity to a track that though much maligned, remains their most famous composition.

Live performances

Premièred at the Ulster Hall, Belfast, on March 5, 1971. Performed at every gig thereafter. Became the finale of the set from Brussels in 1975 to Berlin in 1980. Post-Zeppelin airings include the Live Aid and Atlantic reunions, plus instrumental versions by Page on the ARMS shows in 1983 and the 'Outrider' tour in 1988. Page employed the opening chords of the song to close the live version of 'Babe I'm Gonna Leave You on their 1995/96 and 1998 Page & Plant world tours. Page & Plant did perform a surprise edited version for a TV appearance in Japan in November 1994

MISTY MOUNTAIN HOP
Page, Plant, Jones

Studios: Headley Grange with The Rolling Stones' Mobile; Olympic, London

A HAPPY up-tempo outing, written and recorded at the Grange, with Jones on electric piano and providing the central riff motif the song revolves around. This is another vintage Zeppelin song of which Plant has not grown tired. He has been more than happy to roll out its nostalgic hippy ideals during the Eighties, both on his solo tours, and at reunions with Page and Jones.

Live performances
Joined the set on the European tour in 1971. Used as a link track for 'Since I've Been Loving You' from the Japan tour in 1972 up to the US tour in 1973. Dropped from the set then, but did reappear at the Copenhagen/Knebworth dates. Post-Zeppelin, it has been played by Plant on his solo tours, with Page at the Atlantic reunion, on a guest spot at Hammersmith in 1988, and at the Knebworth Silver Clef show in 1990. Revived by Page & Plant on their 1998 world tour. Performed by Page with the Black Crowes on their 2000 US tour dates.

FOUR STICKS
Page, Plant

Studios: Headley Grange, with The Rolling Stones' Mobile; Island, London

A DIFFICULT track to record, this required many more takes than usual, and is so called because Bonzo employed the use of four drum sticks to create the relentless rhythm track. This was one of the tracks they recut with members of the Bombay Symphony Orchestra in 1972. It also features Jones on Moog synthesiser. Another song that has enjoyed deserved renewed attention in the 90's being one of the most played Zep numbers on Page & Plant's 1995/96 world tour and still a staple part of Plant's solo live set in 2003.

Live performances
Only documented live Zeppelin performance is on the 1971 European tour in Copenhagen. However Page & Plant revived it at their MTV *Unledded* London filming in 1994 and performed it extensively on their 1995/6 world tour. Performed by Plant on his 2002/3 tour with Strange Sensation.

GOING TO CALIFORNIA
Page, Plant

Studios: Headley Grange with The Rolling Stones' Mobile; Olympic

A NOTHER acoustic beauty with some memorable Plant lyrics, heavily influenced by Joni Mitchell. This started out life as a song about Californian earthquakes and when Jimmy, Andy Johns and Peter Grant travelled to LA to mix the album, lo and behold the mountains did begin to tremble and shake. Then it

Led Zeppelin at the start of their career, clockwise from top left:
Jimmy Page, Robert Plant, John Bonham and John Paul Jones.

Jones, Plant, Bonham and Page in 1971.

Led Zeppelin I (March, 1969) and *II* (October, 1969)

Led Zeppelin III (October, 1970) and *IV* (November 1971)

Led Zeppelin in 1969.

Led Zeppelin backstage at the Bath Festival, June 1970.

Clockwise, from top left: Page, Jones, Bonham and Plant.

Robert Plant on stage in 1975.

Houses Of The Holy
(March 1973).

Jimmy Page on stage, 1977.

Physical Graffiti
(February 1975).

John Paul Jones on stage, 1977.

Backstage at the Bath Festival, June 1970.

was known as 'Guide To California'. It also tells of an unrequited search for the ultimate lady. "It's infinitely hard," Plant would often ad lib in the live rendition. Some 20 years later he gave an indication that his own search was ongoing, stating, "Do you know what – it's still hard..." during the Knebworth 1990 show.

Live performances

Introduced on the spring UK tour in 1971. Retained for all shows up to the next year's US tour. Returned to the set for Earls Court, and the 1977 US tour. Performed on Plant's solo tours during 1988,1993 and 2002 and at the Knebworth Silver Clef show in 1990. Revived by Page & Plant on their 1995/96 and 1998 world tours.

WHEN THE LEVEE BREAKS
Page, Plant, Jones, Bonham, Minnie.

Studios: Headley Grange Hampshire with The Rolling Stones' Mobile; Sunset Sound, Los Angeles

ON JUNE 18,1929, in New York, Memphis Minnie and Kansas Joe McCoy recorded a blues tune called 'When The Levee Breaks'. Forty years later in leafy Hampshire, Led Zeppelin reconstructed the song to form the spiralling finale of their fourth album. It had already been tried unsuccessfully at Island at the beginning of the sessions but in Headley Grange it took on a whole new direction.

'Levee' goes down in the annals of Zeppelin history for Bonzo's crushing drum sound performed, according to Page, on a brand new kit that had only just been delivered from the factory. Engineer Andy Johns has revealed that the unique drum sound came about after Bonzo complained that he wasn't getting the sound he wanted. Johns promptly repositioned the kit in the Headley Grange hallway and hung two M1160 mikes from the staircase. Back in the Stones mobile he compressed the drum sound through two channels and added echo through Jimmy's Binson echo unit. The result was the most sampled and envied drum track in rock history. Beyond the millennium it can be heard spinning amongst DJ turntables the world over as a perennial mixing backing track.

Alongside that drum sound, Page contributes a rampant bottleneck guitar, while Plant blows a mean mouth harp that cleverly winds it all up in a barrage of backwards echo.

Live performances

Rehearsed for the 1975 tour itinerary, it was tried out at the Rotterdam and Brussels warm up dates, but survived only a handful of opening shows on the subsequent US tour before being discarded. Page and Plant revived it at their Corris Slate location MTV *Unledded* filming in 1994 and on their 1995/6 world tour. Performed in an instrumental version by John Paul Jones on his 1999/2001 tour dates.

Houses Of The Holy

Atlantic K50014 | UK Album Chart: No 1: US: No 1

MUCH OF **L**ED **Z**EPPELIN'S **FIFTH ALBUM WAS RECORDED AT** **S**TARGROVES, Mick Jagger's country estate in Berkshire, in the spring of 1972. Both Jimmy and John Paul had by now installed home studios of their own, enabling them to demo their own songs, and Jimmy was therefore able to present complete arrangements of 'The Rain Song' with its strange tunings and *chiaroscuro* dynamics, and another guitar extravaganza then known as 'Over The Hills'. Jones, meanwhile, had honed 'No Quarter', a track first tried out earlier at Headley Grange, into a brooding, quivering, synth-styled mantra.

Once installed in Stargroves other songs came from rehearsing together. These sessions on location, together with a further bout of recording at Olympic in May, proved so productive that some numbers didn't even make the final *Houses Of The Holy* line-up. 'Black Country Woman', 'Walter's Walk', 'The Rover' and even the title track would all appear on later Led Zeppelin albums.

Following the overdubbing sessions at Olympic, Zeppelin commenced another extensive American tour. Along the way Eddie Kramer booked more time at Electric Lady studios in New York where Jimi Hendrix had once held court. It's rumoured that during these sessions the group committed to tape a series of rock'n'roll classics, including most of the tracks on Elvis' *Gold Records Volume I* which they liked to play at sound checks before concerts.

It's been suggested that Jimmy wasn't as happy with the overall sound from Stargroves compared to that at Headley Grange. This I find surprising. There's a confidence and maturity about the *Houses* album that accounted for a notable progression in their ensemble playing. "I can remember Bonzo, Plant, Page and Jones out on the lawn listening to playbacks of 'D'yer Mak'er' and 'Dancing Days' all walking like Groucho Marx in sync, with back steps and forward steps in time to the music," recalls Eddie Kramer and these tracks in particular vividly illustrated the good to be alive feel of the period.

Houses Of The Holy ushered in the golden middle period of Zeppelin supremacy. By the time of its release on March 26, 1973, Led Zeppelin were unquestionably the most popular live band in America and probably the world. Along with The Rolling Stones and The Who, they formed a mighty triumvirate of great British bands who bestrode the rock concert industry like colossi.

After the usual long delay due to the inevitable sleeve problems,

Houses tied in nicely with a tour of Europe that was closely followed with a two-legged assault on America. In fact the week the album ascended to the top of the American chart, Led Zeppelin opened their US tour by playing two mammoth dates. In Atlanta they drew 49,000 on May 4, while the next day a staggering 56,800 packed into the Tampa stadium in Florida. This gave them the distinction of attracting the largest audience ever for a single act performance, beating the previous record held by The Beatles for their Shea Stadium show. It was a record that they themselves would top at the Silverdome Pontiac four years later.

Houses Of The Holy had been recorded almost a year previously, and much of the material had been tested on audiences across the US, Japan, the UK and Europe during 1972/3. It was first touted for release early in January, when it was known as *Led Zeppelin V*. The delays came with the sleeve. This time they chose a collage print depicting a group of children mysteriously scaling the top of a mountain, which, according to Page, denoted the feeling of expectancy for the music contained within.

The distinctive sleeve design was the product of a meeting between the Hipgnosis sleeve design team and Jimmy, Robert and Peter Grant. Aubrey Powell of Hipgnosis recalls that both Peru and Ireland were considered for location shooting, with the Giant's Causeway in Ireland eventually being chosen. Powell took two children along and based his image on a science fiction book called *Childhood's End*.

The outer photos were shot in black and white in appaling conditions while the inner sleeve was taken at a nearby castle. All the shots were later airbrushed, though original instructions for the children to be gold and silver were amended by accident to a more atmospheric purple. The shots with the two children were multi-printed to create the effect of 11 nubiles that adorned the finished article.

This elaborate printing technique delayed the original January 5 release date to late March. Following in the tradition of the fourth album, it was an artistic statement that gave little indication of the musical content within. This, of course, only added to Led Zeppelin's increasing mystique. Given the minimal approach of modern day CD packaging, the *Houses* sleeve remains a shining example of the gloriously self-indulgent nature of Seventies album cover artwork.

After the furore of the wordless fourth album, Grant did allow Atlantic to add a wrap-around band to UK copies of the sleeve. Surprisingly, this tactic survived well into the Eighties. However, the CD version does have the title logos printed on the cover itself, a further indication of the lack of quality control applied when the original CDs were issued.

Despite receiving some decidedly mixed reviews, the album entered the UK chart at number one, while in America its 39-week run on the *Billboard* Top 40 was their longest since the first album.

Certain press criticism was levelled at the tongue-in-cheek nature of tracks such as 'The Crunge' and 'D'yer Mak'er'. Once again they had not travelled down the expected path, and in pleasing themselves they may have not pleased the critics. But their ever increasing following, as the 1973 US tour testified, was still with them every step of the way. In retrospect, *Houses Of The Holy* holds its ground with the middle period releases quite admirably. The barnstorming effect of the early era was now levelling off and though devoid of the electricity of *Led Zeppelin I* and *II*, or the sheer diversity of the third album, and lacking the classic status of the fourth, Houses took stock of their situation. In doing so, it laid several foundations on which they would expand their future collective musical aspirations.

THE SONG REMAINS THE SAME
Page, Plant

Studios: Stargroves, Berkshire, with The Rolling Stones' Mobile; Olympic, London

THIS shimmering Page extravaganza was originally conceived as an instrumental under the working title 'Plumpton And Worcester Races'. When Plant added the lyrics, it took on the working title of 'The Campaign'. The finished article is an uplifting barrage of six-stringed picking and chording, over which Plant's slightly speeded-up vocal track chronicles their travels and observes that the common denominator to it all is that if you give, you get back, in fact 'The Song Remains The Same'. Another track that Jimmy transferred to the Gibson doubleneck to play live, in the studio he overdubs on Telecaster, and a Rickenbacker 12-string. John Paul Jones also puts in some wonderful bass lines.

Live performances
Premièred on the Japanese tour in October 1972. Retained for every live gig up to Earls Court in 1975. This arrangement always dove-tailed into its studio counterpart 'The Rain Song'. From the US tour in 1977 up to the 1979 Copenhagen and Knebworth shows, the track was employed as a vibrant set opener in its own right. It was then rested for the Europe dates. Revived by Page & Plant on their 1995/96 world tour.

THE RAIN SONG
Page, Plant

Studios: Stargroves with The Rolling Stones' Mobile; Olympic; Electric Lady

THIS was one of the new songs for Houses that benefited from the recent installation of a studio console at Jimmy's Plumpton home. A new Vista model, it was partly made up from the Pye Mobile Studio which had been used to record the group's 1970 Albert Hall show and The Who's *Live At Leeds* album.

Page was able to bring in a completed arrangement of the melody for which Robert matched some sensitive lyrics. This track also marks the début of the John Paul Jones one-man orchestra. He layers on a drifting string symphony created by a mellotron, an early sampling keyboard synth. Page plays his Dan Electro guitar here. The working title for this song was 'Slush', a reference to its easy listening mock orchestral arrangement.

Live performances
Came into the set as a dual performance with 'The Song Remains The Same'. Retained in this format on every subsequent tour up to Earls Court in 1975. When 'The Song' became the set opener, 'The Rain Song' was dropped for the 1977 dates. However, it was revived as a solo piece for the Copenhagen, Knebworth and Europe 1979/80 gigs. Another number which required the Gibson double-neck guitar on stage. Revived by Page & Plant at their MTV *Unledded* London filming in 1994 and on the Japanese/Australian leg of their 1995/96 world tour.

OVER THE HILLS AND FAR AWAY
Page, Plant

Studios: Stargroves with The Rolling Stones' Mobile; Electric Lady

OPENS with some superbly interwoven acoustic playing, before shifting gear for an electric chorus that finds the Jones/Bonham rhythm bond steadfast as ever. Plant waxes hippily about that open road (and that Acapulco gold). A cut that displays all the colour and light of the group's maturing musical landscape.

Archive footage of this track being performed live at Seattle in 1977 and Knebworth in 1979 was used for an officially distributed video of the song used to promote the 1990 *Remasters* releases.

Live performances
One of the new songs to be introduced on stage way ahead of the album's release. This track came in on the 1972 US trip. Usually employed in the early part of the set to provide Page with a chance to warm up the Gibson, it stayed with them for each tour up to the Copenhagen/Knebworth shows in 1979. Performed by Jimmy on his solo Outrider tour in 1988. Revived by Page & Plant on three occasions on their 1995/6 world tour.

THE CRUNGE
Bonham, Jones, Page, Plant

Studios: Stargroves with The Rolling Stones' Mobile; Olympic; Electric Lady

'THE Crunge' came out of a Bonham inspired spontaneous jam at Stargroves. Jimmy came in with a funk riff (and a chord sequence he'd had kicking around since 1970), stepping on and off the beat, rendering the whole thing completely undanceable. This spurred Robert to come up with a set of lyrics that parodied the James Brown/'Take it to the bridge' school of funk mannerisms. With tongue firmly planted in cheek, they named this non-dance cult 'The Crunge' and even thought about illustrating the 'dance steps' on the cover. Maybe the critics would then have seen the joke. Incidentally, that's Jimmy and engineer George Chkianz you can hear talking, just as Bonzo comes in on the intro.

Live performances

Never performed as a track in its own right, 'The Crunge' was incorporated firstly during 'Dazed And Confused' on the 1972 US tour, and more commonly within 'Whole Lotta Love' up to the 1975 dates. It was mainly put in as an ad libbed instrumental though on occasions did receive a full Plant vocal, notably on the March 24/25 1975 LA Forum dates where on the latter night it was sequenced together with James Brown's 'Sex Machine'. A bootleg from this gig was entitled 'Sex Machine And The Butter Queen'.

alive' vibe with a smiling vocal, as he sings about those lazy hazy summer nights. It comes as no surprise to hear Eddie Kramer's story of them dancing out on the Stargroves lawn during the playback of this track. It summarises the positive atmosphere of the time perfectly.

This was the first track from the album to be offered for radio play by Atlantic. It was premièred on Saturday March 24, 1973, on the Radio One *Rosko* lunch time show.

Live performances

First aired as early as the first Electric Magic gig at the Wembley Empire Pool on November 20, 1971, it re-emerged during the second half of the 1972 US tour and at the Seattle Coliseum on June 19 when it was played twice: first in the main set, then as an encore! Discarded for the '73 US tour, it made a surprise on the '77 US tour, this time as part of the acoustic medley with 'Bron-Y-Aur Stomp'. A complete acoustic version was also performed at the June 27 Forum show in 1977. Revived by Page & Plant on their 1995/6 world tour.

DANCING DAYS
Page, Plant

Studios: Stargroves with The Rolling Stones' Mobile; Electric Lady

BUILT AROUND another classically incessant Page riff, this is a complete joy from start to finish. Plant captures the intended 'good to be

D'YER MAK'ER
Bonham, Jones, Page, Plant

Studios: Stargroves with The Rolling Stones' Mobile; Electric Lady

ANOTHER number constructed out of rehearsals at Stargroves. Bonzo came up with the song's structure, which set out to capture a

Fifties do-wop feel (hence the Rosie And The Originals sleeve credit) and what began as a mock Fifties spoof à la Ben E. King then twisted into a reggae off beat. By retaining this slight off-beat on the tempo, the subtle reggae influence emerged, which the critics were quick to jump on. Such was the commercial appeal of this track, Robert Plant was keen to issue it as a single in the UK. Atlantic even went as far as distributing advance promo copies to DJs, but the others did not share Plant's enthusiasm for its release. The promo copies have become much sought after Zeppelin collectables. 'D'Yer Mak'er' remained on the album only, its old English music hall joke title destined to confuse our American cousins, while the music profiled Bonzo at his very best.

'D'Yer Mak'er' seems to have become a controversial issue within the band. Jones has asserted his disdain for the number, feeling it started off as a joke and wasn't thought through carefully enough.

Live performances
Though never performed live in its entirety, Plant did throw in lines from the song during the 'Whole Lotta Love' medley *circa* 1973/75, notably at the March 21 date in Hamburg on the 1973 European tour and final night at Earls Court on May 25, 1975.

NO QUARTER
Jones. Page, Plant

Studios: Stargroves with The Rolling Stones' Mobile; Olympic; Electric Lady

---

THIS brooding Jones creation had been tried a year earlier at Headley Grange. Now slowed down in tempo, and with added synth, bass and piano effects, it took on a dark mysterious texture. Plant's vocals are superbly treated, while the instrumental passage, where Jones' grand piano merges with Page and Bonham's understated rhythmic touches, is a sequence of high drama and quite breathtaking in its delivery.

One of their foremost studio achievements, outtake versions that have emerged on the bootleg CD *Studio Daze* offer much insight into the song's construction and again demonstrate Bonzo's vital contribution to the feel of the track. On the instrumental backing track outtakes he lays down exquisite spacey snare fills for Jimmy and Jonesy to work around. The guitar solo effect was achieved by direct injunction and compression.

Live performances
Not surprisingly this particular journey became a centrepiece of their live shows. Thus from its introduction to the set on the 1973 US tour, it developed into a marathon Jones showcase, played at every show through to Knebworth in 1979. At the LA Forum on March 25,

1975, Page, Jones and Bonham took the song into a very atypical jazz arrangement quite unlike any other version in that era, and during 1977 live versions of the song included a full version of B. Bumble & The Stingers' 'Nut Rocker'. It was deleted from the set on the scaled down Europe shows of 1980. Plant re-introduced the number to his 'Manic Nirvana' tour in 1990. The arrangement on this occasion, however, did not remain the same. Revived by Page & Plant at their MTV *Unledded* location filming in Dolgoth Wales in 1994 and on their 1995/6 and 1998 world tours. Performed in an instrumental version by John Paul Jones on his 1999 tour dates.

Page and Co meanwhile strut out another memorable riff that would later inspire a few thousand sales of Beastie Boys albums. The closing do-wop finale is a further joy. "So good!" shouts Plant and he's so right. The live performance of this track drawn from their 1973 Madison Square Garden gigs is one of the stand out moments from the 2003 Led Zeppelin DVD set.

Live performances

This high energy outing came into the set as early as the 1972 summer tour. It was an encore during the UK tour dates of 1973. It was further employed on the European trek in the spring, and the summer tour of the US. Deleted thereafter. During Plant's solo tours samples of the track and the 'la-la-la-la-la-la' chorus were inserted into 'Tall Cool One'. Page quoted from the song's riff during his live version of 'Custard Pie' on the 1988 Outrider tour.

THE OCEAN
Bonham, Jones, Page, Plant

Studios: Stargroves with The Rolling Stones' Mobile; Olympic; Electric Lady

"

WE'VE done four already but now we're steady and then they went..." John Bonham's thick Midlands accent rings in this delightful closing rocker. Just as the title of the song had been a Plant metaphor for the sea of heads he faced in the auditoriums they were now filling, 'The Ocean' refers to Zeppelin's ever growing and ever faithful army of fans. "Has the ocean lost its way, I don't think so," he reflects, going on to explain his devotion to baby Carmen ("She is only three-years old").

Physical Graffiti

Swan Song SSK 89400 | UK Album Chart: No 1; US: No 1

FOR THEIR INAUGURAL SWAN SONG RELEASE, LED ZEPPELIN FINALLY SUCCUMBED to the double album format. A combination of new material recorded early in 1974 at Headley Grange, coupled with a summary of strong material from previous sessions, made up the contents of this blockbuster release.

After the hugely successful 1973 American tour, Led Zeppelin unwound, did some home movie work for their film, and took their time approaching their next recording sessions. It wasn't until November that they returned to Headley Grange with Ronnie Lane's mobile studio for location recording, but the sessions came to a halt fairly quickly and the time was given over to Bad Company, also managed by Peter Grant. At the time the reason given was that John Paul Jones was ill, but it later emerged that Jones had wanted to quit the band as he was fed up with touring. He even suggested – somewhat tongue-in-cheek – that he's been offered a position as choirmaster at Winchester Cathedral. Peter Grant urged caution, suggesting that Jones was overwrought from the incessant touring and should take a rest from Zeppelin for a few weeks. Jones changed his mind and sessions resumed at Headley Grange after the Christmas holidays.

Once re-united, it was a case of pooling ideas. Mostly what they had were, as Robert later described them, 'the belters'. "We got eight tracks off," he explained in the spring of 1974, "and a lot of them are really raunchy. We did some real belters with live vocals, off-the-wall stuff that turned out really nice."

Similar to the sessions for the previous two albums, the location recording technique gave them ample time to develop material along the way. Plant again: "Some of the tracks we assembled in our own fashioned way of running through a track and realising before we knew it that we had stumbled on something completely different."

A distinct character of these sessions is the throatiness of Robert's vocals. Talking to *The Scotsman* newspaper in 1988, Plant said: "Fifteen years ago I had an operation on my throat and couldn't speak for three weeks." If Robert had got his dates right, the period he was talking about was the autumn/winter of 1973/4, and this may explain why his voice was less than crystal clear for the sixth album sessions.

Those eight tracks, engineered by Ron Nevison, extended beyond the length of a conventional album and this prompted them to construct a double set. This was achieved by re-assessing the material recorded for earlier albums, from which seven further tracks were added. The whole package was mixed down by the late Keith Harwood at Olympic, and released as *Physical Graffiti* in 1975. It was a massive outpouring of Zeppelin music that proved to be the definitive summary of their studio work.

The sleeve design is one of their most elaborate. The front cover depicts a New York tenement block (actual location: 96 St. Marks, NYC), through which interchanging window illustrations reveal such candid shots as the group dressed in drag, and Bonzo in tights for the Roy Harper St. Valentines Day gig.

The title *Physical Graffiti* was coined by Page to illustrate the whole physical and written energy that had gone into producing the set. The release date was timed to coincide with their 1975 tour campaign which commenced in America in January. Minor delays kept it from appearing until late February. When it did appear the demand was staggering.

Physical Graffiti made what had by now become Led Zeppelin's customary entry at number one on the UK chart, while America just went *Graffiti* mad. It entered every US chart at number three, then a record for a new entry, before lodging itself at the top for six weeks. Even more remarkable was the fact all five previous Zepp albums returned to the *Billboard* chart. No other rock act had ever been so well represented.

It had been two years since their last album, but the waiting had been worth it. Led Zeppelin had delivered. It still stands as their finest recorded achievement. Given the luxury of the double format, *Physical Graffiti* mirrors every facet of the Zeppelin repertoire. The end result is a finely balanced embarrassment of riches. Through light and shade, from a whisper to a scream, this one has it all.

IN 1997 A 33 MINUTE TAPE OF OUTTAKES FROM *PHYSICAL GRAFFITI* EMERGED via various bootleg labels. Alongside alternate mixes of 'Trampled Underfoot' and 'Custard Pie', it includes an instrumental run through of 'Kashmir' and a full alternate version of 'In The Light' with different lyrics and keyboard parts. It also has two takes of the often talked about Page instrumental opus Swan Song -originally planned to be the album's title track. This meandering Page virtuoso piece has a chord progression later used on 'Ten Years Gone' but remained unfinished. Years later Page did use elements of the track in the Firm composition 'Midnight Moonlight' and on the live version of the track premiered on the US leg of the ARMS tour when it was performed with Paul Rodgers under the title 'Bird On A Wing'.

CUSTARD PIE
Page, Plant

Studios: Headley Grange with Ronnie Lane's Mobile; Olympic

ONE OF THE belters from Headley Grange, 'Custard Pie' is a prime knockabout rocker with a vintage Page riff, finely undercut by J.P. on clavinet. As well as tapping the Bukka White songbook for the 'shake 'em on down' refrain, other sources of inspiration can be traced to Sonny Boy Fuller's 'Custard Pie Blues', Blind Boy Fuller's 'I Want Some Of Your Custard Pie' and Big Joe Williams' version of the song, 'Drop Down Mama'. Plant throws in a bluesy mouth harp to aid the effect, Page filters a piercing solo through an ARP synthesiser, and it all dances off to a pleasing fade. 'Drop down!' squeals Plant and Bonzo duly obliges with a typically robust attack on the bass drum.

Live performances
Although rehearsed for the 1975 set, 'Custard Pie' never received a public Zeppelin airing. Years later, Plant would redress the balance by incorporating a chorus of the song on the end of the live version of 'Tall Cool One'. Page also produced his own live version on the Outrider tour the same year. It was also performed at the Jason Bonham wedding reunion in 1990. Revived by Page & Plant on their 1995/6 tour. Performed by Page and the Black Crowes on their 1999 US tour.

THE ROVER
Page, Plant

Studios: Stargroves, Berkshire, with The Rolling Stones' Mobile; Olympic

A TRACK that dates back to 1970, 'The Rover' was rehearsed as an acoustic blues piece before being recorded at Stargroves with Eddie Kramer for the fifth album. When it didn't make the final 'Houses Of The Holy' selection, Page returned to it in 1974, overdubbing and re-mixing the basic track with Keith Harwood. The curious "Guitar lost courtesy Nevison... Salvaged by the grace of Harwood" sleeve credit would appear to be a reference to certain mixing difficulties they may have had here – Nevison being engineer Ron Nevison.

'The Rover' possesses a stirring melodic base, from which Plant waxes idealistically about the need for solidarity, and Page strings together one of his most perfectly constructed solos.

Live performances
Though elements of the song were heard on stage during 1972 and 1977, no complete version was ever played. However, the song was rehearsed in full, as can be heard on the remarkable soundcheck rehearsal tape recorded on July 6 at the Chicago Auditorium and now available on the bootleg CDs *Round And Round* and *Tribute To Johnny Kidd And The Pirates*. The rehearsal took place before the opening date of the second half of the tour. "In

those days we used to play songs that were totally unrelated to the current tour during rehearsals. In fact, loads of songs were born in the rehearsal jam session," Page said in 1990. Used as an insert occasionally during Babe I'm Gonna Leave You by Page & Plant on their 1995/96 tour.

IN MY TIME OF DYING
Bonham, Jones, Page, Plant

Studios: Headley Grange with Ronnie Lane's Mobile, Olympic

A TRADITIONAL song that can be found on Bob Dylan's first album, Zeppelin's arrangement came together during the initial sixth album sessions in 1974. The lyrics can be traced back to a 1927 recording by Blind Willie Johnson entitled 'Jesus Make Up My Dying Bed'. With one of the most powerful drum sounds ever committed to tape (recorded in the same way as 'When The Levee Breaks'), the point where Page straps in for a peerless bottleneck frenzy backed by Jones and Bonzo at the nerve centre, has to be one of the most scintillating moments in the whole of the Zeppelin catalogue. The intensity is quite frightening. It eventually winds down via a studio cough from Bonzo. "That's gotta be the one hasn't it?" inquires the drummer from behind the screens. Indeed it was...

A stunning live delivery of this track drawn from their May 1975 Earl's Court shows can be seen on the 2003 Led Zeppelin DVD.

Live performances
Brought in to the revamped set for all their 1975 dates and used again on some of the 1977 US tour where it was alternated with 'Over The Hills And Far Away'. It was a number that Plant was unsure of performing after his 1975 car crash, due to its fatalistic lyrical theme. Post Zep performed by Page on his solo Outrider tour and with David Coverdale on their tour of Japan in 1993. Also with the Black Crowes on their 1999/2000 US tour. Performed by Plant occasionally on his 1993 US tour. Plant did insert lines from the song within the 'Calling To You'/'Whole Lotta Love' medleys on their 1995/6 world tour and within 'How Many More Times' on their 1998 world tour.

HOUSES OF THE HOLY
Page, Plant

Studios: Olympic; Electric Lady

A NOTHER fifth album overspill, this title track was recalled for the double set and required no further re-mixing, having been tied up by Eddie Kramer as far back as the Electric Lady sessions in June 1972. A strident mid-tempo exercise with the same smiling friendliness in its grooves as can be heard on 'Dancing Days'. This similarity may have accounted for its absence on the *Houses Of The Holy* album. In order to create the layered guitar intro and fade, Jimmy used a Delta T digital delay unit.

Live performances

Never performed live by Zeppelin. Plant did occasionally sing lines from the song within an arrangement of Garnet Mimms As Long As I Have You on his Priory of Brion gigs in 2000.

TRAMPLED UNDERFOOT
Jones, Page, Plant

Studios: Headley Grange with Ronnie Lane's Mobile; Olympic

MUCH rehearsal went into perfecting the relentless semi-funk riff that dominates this driving tale of the motor car and its relation with the sexual act, a theme explored by Robert Johnson in 'Terraplane Blues'. Jones' clavinet and Jimmy's wah-wah and backwards echo make for a formidable partnership. Plant's vocals are a little too back in the mix (a characteristic of most of the Headley Grange tracks) but not enough to dim the overall incessant effect, which remains quite irresistible. Special UK singles of this track were pressed for promotional purposes in time for the Earls Court shows.

Live performances

Another Zeppelin concert showpiece, this track was played on every live show from 1975 through to the last gig in Berlin in 1980. For some of the 1977 US shows it became an encore number. In 1988 it was revived by Plant for his Now And Zen tour, including a memorable performance with Jimmy at Hammersmith in April. Revived by Page & Plant on their 1998 world tour. Performed by John Paul Jones on his 1999 tour dates.

KASHMIR
Bonham, Page, Plant

Studios: Headley Grange with Ronnie Lane's Mobile; Olympic

THIS particular epic grew out of two separate Page riffs which he was unable to combine until he and John Bonham demo'ed it late in 1973. Robert wrote the lyrics on the road to Tan Tan while holidaying in South Morocco immediately after the 1973 US tour, and called it 'Driving To Kashmir' as a working title. He was later to refer to it as 'The Pride of Led Zeppelin'.

When it came to recording in early 1974, J.P. scored a suitable Eastern string arrangement. Kashmir's real beauty of course, lies in Page's Moorish chord riff that carries the song towards those desert wastelands. There is an ethereal, slightly discordant and somewhat eerie quality to this music that hints at the mysteries of the East and seems derived from musical signatures not normally found in the standard Western scale. Page has revealed that outside session musicians were brought in to add strings and horns, a rare occurrence on a Zeppelin session.

Unquestionably the most startling and impressive track on *Physical Graffiti*, and arguably the most progressive and original track that Led Zeppelin ever recorded, 'Kashmir' went a long way towards establishing their credibility with sceptical rock critics. Many regard this track as the finest example of the sheer majesty of Zeppelin's special chemistry. The song enjoyed further success in 1998 when Page utilised the basic riff of 'Kashmir' for a collaboration with rapper Puff Daddy. This new version used on the *Godzilla* soundtrack reached number 2 in the UK singles chart.

Live performances

Made its début in Rotterdam on January 11, 1975. Performed on every subsequent gig up to the final show in Berlin on July 7, 1980. From the 1977 US dates onwards, 'Kashmir' led out of Jimmy's 'White Summer' / 'Black Mountain Side' guitar spot, for which he switched to a Dan Electro guitar. It was aired at the Atlantic Records 21st birthday celebrations at Madison Square Garden. Jimmy also slotted in riffs of this epic during the 'Moonlight Midnight' medley on his Outrider tour and played it with David Coverdale on their Japanese tour in 1993.

Revived by Page & Plant at their *Unledded* London filming in 1994 and on their 1995/96 world tour.

as 'In The Morning'. Opening with a drone-like keyboard effect from Jones, the track travels down more than one tempo change, as Robert sings with passion about the need for eternal optimism. The fade-out 'is another wonderful example of the interplay enjoyed by Jimmy and Bonzo, as a mass of overdubbed guitar parts filter round some exemplary percussion. Reason enough for Jimmy to select this number as his favourite track on the album.

Live performances

Surprisingly enough, this was never attempted live. It was, however, used as an intro link to 'Nobody's Fault But Mine' on some of Plant's Now And Zen American shows in 1988. If 'The 80s Part One' tour had occurred, this would have been a perfect vehicle for Jonesey's 'Dream Machine'. Plant did insert lines from the song within the Calling To You/ Whole Lotta Love medleys performed with Page on their 1995/6 world tour and within How Many More Times on their 1998 world tour. Performed by Page with The Black Crowes on their 2000 US dates. Plant performed the song in full on the Scandinavian and US tour with Strange Sensation in 2001.

IN THE LIGHT
Jones, Page, Plant

Studios: Headley Grange with Ronnie Lane's Mobile; Olympic

'IN THE LIGHT' grew out of a similar-styled rehearsal number known

BRON-Y-AUR
Page

Studios: Island, London; Olympic

A SHORT winsome acoustic solo, written and tried for 'Zeppelin

III'. Later to appear as part of the non-performance soundtrack to *The Song Remains The Same* movie.

Live performances
Briefly part of the acoustic set on the sixth American tour August/September 1970.

DOWN BY THE SEASIDE
Page, Plant

Studios: Island; Olympic

ANOTHER song written at Bron-Y-Aur in the Spring of 1970. Originally conceived as a Neil Young-influenced acoustic strum-along (with Robert playing guitar), this electric arrangement was recorded at the time of the fourth album sessions. It features some lively electric piano, a sensitive Plant vocal, and an unexpected rise in tempo half way through. The manner in which Page and Bonham turn away from the tranquil landscape of the song to take it all up a gear, and then slip back to the original lilting theme with effortless ease, is a master-stroke of controlled dynamics. Plant's lasting affinity for the song led him to record a new version in 1994 with Tori Amos for inclusion on the official Led Zeppelin tribute album *Encomium*.

Live performances
Never performed live by Zeppelin. Plant did insert lines from the song within the Calling To You/Whole Lotta Love medlies with Page on their 1995/6 world tour.

TEN YEARS GONE
Page, Plant

Studios: Headley Grange with Ronnie Lane's Mobile; Olympic

ORIGINALLY a Page instrumental elements of which were sourced from the unreleased track 'Swan Song' (the name they chose for their own record label). A moving Plant narrative about an age old love affair that still cuts deep. The emotional content is further emphasised by Page's subtle touches that colour the song. A series of overdubbed guitar parts in perfect harmony hint at the intention of this track as an instrumental tour-de-force. As it is, it stands as one of their finest arrangements.

Live performances
Brought in for the 1977 US tour. JP originally played the melody on acoustic guitar but then introduced a special three-necked guitar that encompassed bass pedals, mandolin and six- and 12-string acoustics. Played again on the July 24 Copenhagen warm-up show and at the August 4 Knebworth show in 1979. The problems encountered in setting up Jones' multi-faceted instrument probably accounted for its omission at the following week's concert and at the other Copenhagen warm-up. Revived for one performance only by Page & Plant in Osaka Japan on February 15 1996. Performed by Page with the Black Crowes on their 1999 and 2000 US tour dates.

NIGHT FLIGHT
Jones, Page, Plant

Studios: Headley Grange with The Rolling Stones' Mobile; Olympic

A BRIGHT rocker from the sessions at Headley Grange for the fourth album. The lyrics reflected Plant's thoughts on the threat of nuclear war. Plant's strident vocals are crystal clear and supported by some turbulent drumming. Page puts in some swirling Leslie guitar, playing off a warm organ sound supplied by J.P. An outtake with backing vocals on the middle-eight section remains in the vaults. Never played live with Zep, 23 years after it's release Page & Plant finally aired the song live at their low key ULU London show on October 30 1998.

Live performances
Although never played live, it can be heard in a rehearsal version from the July 6 1973 Chicago soundcheck, an arrangement that testifies to its 1971 vintage. The song was revived by Page & Plant on four occasions on their 1998 world tour. Plant also performed it with Strange Sensation on their Scandinavian/US tour in 2001.

THE WANTON SONG
Page, Plant

Studios: Headley Grange with Ronnie Lane's Mobile; Olympic

'THE WANTON Song' is a thrusting Plant tale of carnal delights, ably supported by a devastatingly simple but quite brilliant Page riff that grinds the listener into submission. His guitar effects include the use of backwards echo during the solo and refrain, and also playing through a Leslie speaker to create the organ effect. Jones and Bonham back up with a barrage of noise with equal panache. A reassuringly tough product of the sixth album sessions in 1974.

Live performances
The bridge of the song is another piece of Zeppelin music that can be heard clearly on the Chicago July 6 soundcheck tape. It was played on the European warm up dates in early 1975 and some of the opening 1975 US tour dates and then discarded. Extensively performed by Page & Plant as a set opener on their 1995/6 and 1998 world tours. Performed by Page with the Black Crowes on their 2000 US tour dates.

BOOGIE WITH STU
Bonham, Jones, Page, Plant, Stewart, Mrs Valens

Studios: Headley Grange with the Rolling Stones Mobile; Olympic

A LOOSE jam recorded at the same sessions which produced 'Rock And Roll' for the fourth album. This has Ian Stewart, the Rolling Stones' tour manager and resident boogie-woogie keyboard player, playing barrel-house piano. Heavily based on Richie Valens' Fifties hit 'Ooh My Head' (check out the *La Bamba* movie), hence the credit to his widow. The slapping guitar came from an overdub session with the ARP guitar synth. Robert came up with a working title 'Sloppy Drunk'.

Live performances
Never performed live.

BLACK COUNTRY WOMAN
Page, Plant

Studios: The garden at Stargroves with The Rolling Stones' Mobile; Olympic

EVER ON the look-out for off-the-wall recording locations (Plant once tried to record some vocals out in the quadrangle of Headley Grange and had to flee from a gaggle of geese that attacked him!), the boys took to the garden at Stargroves for this session in the spring of 1972. The resulting take was nearly shelved when a plane cruised overhead, but as the opening dialogue reveals, it was all captured for posterity. Prior to release 'Black Country Woman' was subtitled 'Never Ending Doubting Woman Blues'. This was a reference to a final spoken tag left off the finished version which had Robert proclaiming, "What's the matter with you mama, never-ending, nagging, doubting woman blues."

Live performances
This was performed at one show at least in America in 1972. It was then merged into a medley with 'Bron-Y-Aur Stomp' for the 1977 US dates.

Revived by Plant on his 1988 *Now And Zen* tour.

SICK AGAIN
Page, Plant

Studios: Headley Grange with Ronnie Lane's Mobile; Olympic

AND FINALLY... a mid tempo-rocker based on Plant's still vivid tales of the 1973 US tour and the ladies that surrounded them. It's powered by a series of Page runs and some ferocious Bonham hammering that assist in conjuring up the required images. Juicy and muscular and inevitably tight but loose, 'Sick Again' is a fitting exit. Listen carefully and you can hear Bonzo coughing out loud after Page's sonic finale. The live performance of this track drawn from their Knebworth 1979 shows is another stand out moment of the 2003 DVD release.

Live performances
Held the distinction of being the second number performed on all the 1975 and 1977 tour dates. On the 1977 tour it was preceded by a link from 'The Rover'. It was rehearsed at Bray Studios during the summer of 1979 for its return to the set but it only made three out of the four 79 shows. It's likely it was exorcised from the first Copenhagen warm up show due to the late running because of a power failure. Performed by Page with the Black Crowes on their 1999 and 2000 US tour dates.

Presence

Swan Song SSK 59402 | UK Album Chart: No 1; US: No 1

AND THEN THERE WAS *PRESENCE*. FORCED BY PLANT'S CAR SMASH TO CANCEL A projected world tour due to commence on August 23, 1975, the group wisely used this convalescent period to write and record a new album.

The seeds of this album can be traced back to when Page joined Plant recuperating in Malibu (which explains why most of the album consists solely of Page/Plant compositions). Robert had already written some reflective lyrics and coupled with Page's input, these fragments of songs were soon under rehearsal as Jones and Bonham flew over for pre-production sessions at Hollywood's SIR rehearsal studios. After a month of rehearsals, the group were anxious to record. Musicland Studios in Munich (a favourite Page haunt) was their next destination. In the fastest time since the first album, seven tracks were laid down in a period of just three weeks.

"I think it was just a reflection of the total anxiety and emotion of the period," Page said at the time. "There's a hell of a lot of spontaneity about that album. We went in with virtually nothing and everything just came pouring out."

With his partner at less than full fitness, Page took total responsibility for the album's completion. His playing and production dominate the album's seven tracks, and in stark contrast to the relaxed atmosphere of the last four albums, this album came together through intense 18-hour-day sessions. In fact the studio time booked actually overran, forcing Page to borrow two days from the incoming Rolling Stones, during which time he completed the album's overdubs. (When Page politely requested the extra time from Mick Jagger, the venerable Stone was reportedly amazed that Zeppelin had put their album together so quickly and that Jimmy required only *two* extra days for overdubs. Rolling Stones' albums, it seems, took many months to complete.)

The album was completed on November 27, the day before Thanksgiving. An ecstatic Plant called Swan Song the next day and suggested the album be named *Thanksgiving*. However meetings with sleeve designers Hipgnosis dictated otherwise. Speaking of the powerful force and presence they felt surrounded the group, Page briefed them to come up with a sleeve that displayed this. The bizarre result, a series of *Life* magazine prints of everyday events, mostly involving conservative looking families from middle-America during the Fifties, interrupted by the 'presence' in the form of a mysterious black obelisk (The Object), confused both media and enthusiasts alike. At one stage the plan was to dub the album *Obelisk*. Page held out for *Presence*.

As ever, the sleeve caused delays and it was eventually released in early April 1976. The promotion for the album centred around The Object, the weird obelisk depicted on the cover. In Britain it attained one of the highest ever advance orders, shipping gold on the day of release. In America it leapt from 24 to number one inside two weeks.

Long term, *Presence* was not one of Zeppelin's biggest sellers. Somewhat overshadowed by the late 1976 release of their movie and soundtrack, it has become a much underrated element of their catalogue. The basic drums-bass-guitars formula may lack the diversity of previous Zeppelin sets, but in terms of sheer energy, *Presence* packs a considerable punch, and has emerged as one of their most potent performances. It was the state-of-the-art multi-dubbing facility at the Musicland studio console that accounted for 'Achilles Last Stand', a major Zeppelin opus and a track that excited Plant so much during playback that he fell over and nearly reopened his wounds from the car crash in Greece.

This album is also a triumph for Jimmy Page. His production and dominant guitar style has an urgency and passion that reflects the troubled period that the group were going through at the time. *Presence* is Led Zeppelin with their backs against the wall. As Page once put it, "We started screaming in rehearsals and never stopped."

ACHILLES LAST STAND
Page, Plant

Studio: Musicland, Munich

'ACHILLES Last Stand' is a glorious 10-minute opening salvo that finds all the musicians pushing their talents to the limit. John Bonham's drumming is at once both explosive and inventive, driven along by an irresistible chugging Jones bass line. All this acts as a perfect lynchpin for Page to weave his magic. His playing, constantly overdubbed, is simply magnificent, scaling the song's basic two pronged structure with amazing dexterity. Robert meanwhile unravels a bizarre tale inspired by his and Page's travels across Africa immediately after the Earls Court shows. With its theme of movement, meeting and positive outlook, his lyrics act as a perfect foil for the relentless pace of the track.

'Achilles Last Stand' is an absolutely crucial performance and one that remains as vital today as it did when it took shape inside Musicland back in 1975. A definitive Led Zeppelin yardstick.

Live performances
The first number to be rehearsed when they regrouped in late 1976 for the 1977 US tour, 'Achilles' held its place in the set through 1977, Copenhagen and Knebworth 1979 and right up to the last night of the Over Europe tour. Strangely, it was omitted from what was to be their

final show in Berlin. Page expected to use the Gibson double-neck when it came to performing this epic live, but found it worked fine with just the Gibson Les Paul. Revived by Page & Plant for two performances only on the 1995 US tour.

FOR YOUR LIFE
Page, Plant

Studio: Musicland

MUCH TO admire here both lyrically and musically. Built on a grinding penetrating riff, it finds Plant in understandably reflective mood. "In the pits you go no lower, the next stop's underground," he observes, a phrase that hints at this composition's Malibu period origin. Much of the basic track was created inside Musicland. The simply stunning solo (one of his absolute best) from Page marks the recorded début of a new part of his guitar arsenal – a 1962 Lake Placid blue Fender Stratocaster (supplied by ex-Byrd Gene Parsons), later to be employed on stage during 1979/80 and with The Firm. Not instantly appealing, 'For Your Life' seeps into the consciousness with repeated hearings. One of their most underrated performances.

Live performances
Never performed live. Page did rehearse the song in an instrumental arrangement for the Japanese tour with David Coverdale in 1993 but it was not performed live.

ROYAL ORLEANS
Bonham, Jones, Page, Plant

Studio: Musicland

ROYAL ORLEANS is the name of a hotel in New Orleans located at 621 St Louis Street which was often favoured by the group in their touring heyday and is the setting for this whimsical 'road fever' lament. It tells the tale of 'a man I know' (whose initials were rumoured to be JPJ) whose association with the local clientele provided something of a surprise.

Listen carefully at the end for a great reference to that old soul-swayer Barry White. All this is played out against a short, sharp riff injection, from which Page throws in some funky lines and Bonzo takes to the bongos. 'Royal Orleans'' 'road fever' lyrical content would suggest it was a composition that Plant had written some time previous to this period.

When the entire *Presence* album was premièred on the Alan Freeman show on Radio One on April 3, 1976, the version of this track had an edit in the middle of the solo. This could have been cut to accommodate radio timings, or perhaps this version was taken from an early mix of the album used for pre-release promotion.

Live performances
Never performed live.

NOBODY'S FAULT BUT MINE
Page, Plant

Studio: Musicland

A FULL-BLOODED blues/rock stomper that opens with some suitable sonic embellishments from Jimmy. The up front preening of Page and Plant are duly supported on the flanks by some steadfast rhythm work by J. P. and Bonzo, who handle the stop-go interludes with masterful restraint. Plant blows a mean harmonica before yet another stirring Page onslaught. All in all, a great throwback to some earlier blues-inspired performances. The Page/Plant credit here is a little misleading as Blind Willie Johnson may well have been under the impression that he wrote the lyrics back in 1928, a fact Robert acknowledged when introducing the track on stage in Copenhagen in 1979.

Live performances
A welcome addition to the set on the 1977 US tour. It remained a stage favourite through to the Copenhagen, Knebworth and Europe dates in 1979/80. It was also revived by Plant for his solo tours in 1988 and 1990. Revived by Page & Plant at their *Unledded* location filming at Corris Slate in 1994 and on their 1995/6 world tour. Performed by Page with The Black Crowes on their 1999 and 2000 US tour dates.

CANDY STORE ROCK
Page, Plant

Studio: Musicland

A BASIC Fifties-flavoured rock-'n'roll groove strung along by some Scotty More guitar figures from Page. Heavily echoed Plant vocal in the style of Elvis impersonating Ral Donner, up front bass from J.P. and plenty of timpani in the percussion department add to a performance that years later Plant would acknowledge as one of their very best of the era, "Far beyond the realms of pop, jazz or anything," to quote the man himself.

Live performances
Never performed live by Zeppelin. Page & Plant did perform an ad hoc version at their Wembley Arena gig on July 26 1995. The rockabilly nature of the track finally led Page & Plant to play it in full live at their Montreux Festival appearance during the Night Of Sun Records show on July 7 2001.

HOTS ON FOR NOWHERE
Page, Plant

Studio: Musicland

L IGHT AND airy and vaguely swingish, 'Hots On For Nowhere' delights in its off-the-wall quirkiness. Its basic structure can be traced to the rehearsal sessions for the sixth album as well as the '75 era live versions of 'Dazed And Confused'. Plant unfolds more tales from Malibu, taking a swing at his close friends in the process and throwing in plenty of 'oohs' and 'ahs' for good measure. He later revealed that the accusations levelled at "friends who would give me fuck all" were aimed at Page and Peter Grant who for some reason had incurred his displeasure.

Page meanwhile makes full use of the tremolo arm on the new blue Strat, as he pulls out a ridiculous twang in the middle of a delightful solo. From the moment Plant shouts, "Oh, I lost my way home!" Bonzo roars in with some decorative fills, and Page takes it all out on a blistering babble of notes.

This track's odd time signature was echoed some 18 years later in the impressive Page/David Coverdale collaboration 'Pride And Joy'.

Live performances
Never performed live by Zeppelin. Page did revive the song on his US tour with The Black Crowes in 2000.

being hammered up by Plant with 'Minnie the Moocher' lyrics.

In its completed version 'Tea For One' successfully recaptures the spirit of their earlier, self-penned blues epic 'Since I've Been Loving You'. The solo by Page is beautifully restrained.

Live performances
Never performed live by Zeppelin. Plant would occasionally insert lines from the song within the live version of Since I've Been Loving You during Page & Plant's UK tour in 1995. It was finally given a live airing by Page & Plant on the Japanese leg of their 1995/96 world tour.

NB: The lack of live interpretations of the *Presence* material is quite striking; however, given that it was to be a full year before they returned to the road, perhaps understandable. Had they been able to tour off the back of its release, we may well have enjoyed live takes of 'Candy Store Rock' etc.

TEA FOR ONE
Page, Plant

Studio: Musicland

A RELAXED blues winds up the proceedings. Lyrically Robert reflects on the post accident period when he was separated from his wife Maureen. The track grew out of pre production rehearsals in Hollywood -an early version emerged on a rehearsal tape in the 90's -the basic structure of the song

The Song Remains
The Same

Film Soundtrack

Swan Song 89402 | UK Album Chart: No 1; US: No 2

WITHIN SIX months there was another Zeppelin album in the shops, the soundtrack album to their much maligned feature film.

There had been previous attempts to produce a Led Zeppelin movie before *The Song Remains The Same*. Back in 1970, gigs at the Albert Hall, the spring US tour and a trip to Iceland in June were professionally filmed at the request of manager Peter Grant with a view to assembling an hour-long special for TV distribution. Filming in Japan the next year also took place, but the project never materialised.

The story then shifts to May 1973. Film maker Joe Massot approached Jimmy and Peter during the group's mid-tour break with a view to shooting their return leg. The offer was turned down by Grant who told Massot they had plans to make their own film with a famous director.

However, at the tail end of the two-legged, hugely successful American trip, they changed their minds. A call went out from Grant to Joe Massot on July 14. Massot and crew flew over and filmed various backstage shots, screen tested the stage act at gigs in Baltimore and Pittsburgh and then filmed all three of their Madison Square Garden dates on July 27, 28 and 29. These shows were recorded by Eddie Kramer and formed the basis of the resulting soundtrack album. (All the tracks were later mixed down at Electric Lady in New York and Trident Studios in London.)

Coming at the end of a gruelling tour, these particular performances were hardly magic nights. However, as this was the music that matched the footage, it had to be made available.

There had been plans to shoot some more film on the aborted world tour of 1975/76. After Robert's accident, though, with short term plans for live gigs an impossibility, Page used this period of inactivity to tie up the movie and soundtrack, using the footage shot with Joe Massot and employing Peter Clifton to arrange the technical aspects. The movie poster and sleeve design depicted a run down picture house, which was based on Old Street studios, a London rehearsal theatre they used to perfect the 1973 US stage act prior to touring.

The film was premièred in New York on October 21, with the album hitting the stores the next day. It reached number one in the UK but had to settle for second place in the States. The film went on to become a staple diet of late night movie houses for years to come, and its subsequent issue on video in 1984 has provided a whole new generation of fans with a front row seat on Led Zeppelin.

It has to be said, though, that it's only an adequate representation. Visually and musically their live shows after 1973 were much more spectacular. Indeed, the whole project – film and album – looks somewhat inferior compared to the three-CD *How The West Was Won* set, and the *Led Zeppelin DVD* (see page 79).

The deficiencies of the soundtrack album are best reflected in the decision by Page not to remaster it for CD in the early Nineties. Keen collectors will know of far better material that has surfaced unofficially. In retrospect, performances such as 'Moby Dick' and 'Dazed And Confused' sound somewhat lack-lustre, and the whole question of the actual track listing still baffles. Why, for instance, does 'Celebration Day' appear on the soundtrack album but is nowhere to be seen (or heard) in the film? How come sizzling filmed performances of 'Since I've Been Loving You' and 'Heartbreaker' were somehow left off the album? These anomalies all point to the fact that, as Page admitted at the time, the *Song Remains The Same* movie and soundtrack proved to be rare Led Zeppelin compromises.

All the live material was recorded at Madison Square Garden, New York, on July 27, 28 and 29, 1973, and mixed at Electric Lady, New York, and Trident, London. In compiling the album, Page took differing inserts of songs from the three nights to patch up the best versions.

ROCK AND ROLL
Bonham, Jones, Page, Plant

A FINE opening gambit. For the live version Plant sings in a lower key and Page duck walks into the solo. Vibrant.

CELEBRATION DAY
Jones, Page, Plant

IN THE movie, 'Rock And Roll' is edited into 'Black Dog'. The album, however, has the authentic link into 'Celebration Day'. Strangely edited out of the film, this underrated stage number sounds spot on. Jimmy is particularly impressive weaving a cluster of notes towards the outro. Revives memories of its Knebworth airing.

THE SONG REMAINS THE SAME
Page, Plant

AN EXCELLENT live take with Page switching to the double-neck. In the film, it accompanies Plant's Arthurian fantasy sequence, snippets of which he would later use as a backdrop to 'Immigrant Song' on his 1990 solo tour.

THE RAIN SONG
Page, Plant

DOVETAILS from 'The Song Remains The Same' as was the custom during this era. This version includes some delicate Page strumming and precise Bonham dynamics. At times, though, the mellotron quivers a little unsteadily.

DAZED AND CONFUSED
Page

STRIPPED of the on-stage visuals, this marathon loses its appeal somewhat. There are some high spots, the San Francisco sequence, the bow interlude with its stereo panning and the guitar-vocal interplay. Elsewhere it becomes excessive and lumbering.

NO QUARTER
Jones, Page, Plant

THE ALBUM'S standout performance. Everything works perfectly here, from Jones' revolving opening through to a simply divine Page solo. A slightly different version appears in the film.

STAIRWAY TO HEAVEN
Page, Plant

'STAIRWAY' had yet to take on truly epic proportions during this era, and it followed 'Dazed And Confused' in the set. Such was the excitement of that number, the audience often drowned out the intro to 'Stairway'. Madison Square Garden was one such venue. Though the album version gives little away, the live outtakes reveal Plant trying to settle the audience down. The intro link retained for the album has Plant saying, "This is a song of hope." It edits out his next line: "And it's a very quiet song... so shurrup!"

MOBY DICK
Bonham, Jones, Plant

ANOTHER track that loses most of its impact without the visual footage. In the movie it makes a perfect accompaniment to Bonzo's profile. On record it goes on much too long. A far better idea here would have been to insert the 'Heartbreaker' segment that precedes 'Whole Lotta Love' in the film, run through to the 'Whole Lotta Love' track and then add 'The Ocean' as an encore. Both these tracks were left on the splicing block.

WHOLE LOTTA LOVE
Bonham, Jones, Page, Plant

IN THE film, as in all the shows on the tour, 'Whole Lotta Love' segued in from 'Heartbreaker'. Here it's edited to appear as a track in its own right. Complete with Jimmy on vocals, 'The Crunge' sequence, the theramin attack, and 'Let That Boy Woogie', it sustains the interest. A live version of the re-vamped arrangement they played at Knebworth would be most welcome.

The following tracks appear in the film but not on the record: 'Black Dog', 'Since I've Been Loving You' and 'Heartbreaker'. Jimmy's solo piece from *Physical Graffiti*, 'Bron-Y-Aur', is also heard in the film. Another number, copyrighted as 'Autumn Lake', is played on a hurdy gurdy by Page in an early pre-concert sequence. Songs heard at the Madison Square Garden gigs and likely to have been recorded and filmed include: 'Over The Hills And Far Away', 'Misty Mountain Hop', 'The Ocean', 'Communication Breakdown' and 'Thank You'. 'The Ocean' surfaced on an outtake film track unofficial tape that also has the 'Heartbreaker'/ 'Whole Lotta Love' sequence and takes of 'Stairway To Heaven' and 'Moby Dick'.

In Through The Out Door

Swan Song 59410 | UK Album Chart: No 1; US: No 1

AFTER A TWO-YEAR ABSENCE, DICTATED BY THE TRAGIC DEATH OF ROBERT Plant's young son Karac from a stomach infection, Led Zeppelin finally became active again. This album was recorded at the tail end of 1978 at Abba's Polar Music studio in Stockholm.

Unlike the urgency of Munich in 1975, the Swedish expedition was a much more relaxed affair. Most of the new songs had been well rehearsed in London and there was no need for the studio composing method of earlier recording sessions. They knew what they had to do, and made full use of the studio facilities with Leif Masses and Lennart Ostlund on hand to engineer it all.

The most significant musical contribution came from John Paul Jones. With tongue planted firmly in cheek, he said at the time that his considerable influence on proceedings was due to his arrival at the studio earlier than his colleagues on most days. With lead composing credits on all but one of the seven tracks selected for the album, his contribution was immense.

Rollicking piano on 'South Bound Suarez', an Argentinean soccer burst midway through 'Fool In The Rain', a *Gone With The Wind* string-synth intro for 'I'm Gonna Crawl' and a cluster of classically sounding notes on 'All My Love'—all this was the work of the group's lowest profile member.

The mixing was wrapped up with further sessions in early 1979. There had been talk of a European tour slated for around February. Ultimately they decided to dispense with any conventional gigging (perhaps erroneously), and return to the concert platform in the grandest possible fashion: two shows in August 1979 at the open air Knebworth Park, estimated capacity 300,000 plus.

The completed album, rumoured in some circles to be titled *Look*, was held back from release to coincide with the Knebworth shows. In a rare lapse of marketing strategy, the album missed the concert deadline, appearing a week after Knebworth on August 20. Not that it made a scrap of difference. The record, eventually titled *In Through The Out Door* because, as Jimmy put it, "That's the hardest way to get back in", was rapturously received around the world. It made number one in the UK in its first week and number one in America in its second. It also instantly topped the charts in Japan, New Zealand, Australia and Germany. In the first 10 days of release its sales topped two million.

It was in America though, that the real sales phenomena occurred. Its release was heralded as a saviour to the then flagging US record industry. It generated massive store traffic as it held the top spot for seven weeks. Even more remarkable was the renewed demand for previous Zepp albums. Atlantic shifted a staggering one million back catalogue albums during September 1979, a situation that resulted in Led Zeppelin's entire catalogue appearing on the *Billboard* Top 200 during the weeks of October 27 and November 3. This beat the previous record for most albums on the chart set in 1975 held by... you guessed it, Led Zeppelin.

What made these figures all the more staggering was that during Led Zeppelin's absence from the music scene during the previous two years punk rock had emerged, and a central philosophy of punk was its contrary stance to—and general loathing of—massively popular 'stadium' bands like Led Zeppelin who, it was claimed, were now redundant in the new era. These claims were taken up by newly appointed, young and somewhat hawkish staff at the various UK music magazines, all of which claimed to be arbiters of taste in rock. Such claims might have been fashionable but they were as preposterous as they were premature: it was Led Zeppelin — not the punks — who sold the most records in the new era, just as they had in the old. (It was also Led Zeppelin who won the annual readers' polls in these magazines, much to the chagrin of the editorial staff who championed punk!)

Then there was the album's sleeve. Easily their most ambitious to date, the brief to Hipgnosis was simple enough. They all felt the album to be fresh, new and direct. The album sleeve was to indicate just that. Designer Aubrey Powell felt some of the music had a barrel-house, bayou bar, late night blues feel to it. On Page's suggestion, he worked on a bar room scene, travelling to New Orleans to gain some reference. (Some reports indicate the bar as being the Old Absinthe Bar at 400 Bourbon Street, just around the corner from the Royal Orleans hotel.)

On his return, the Hipgnosis team built a New Orleans bar room scene at Shepperton studios, shooting six different scenes. These sepia-toned photos formed the six alternate sleeves that were issued, each one depicting the view from the six characters in the scene. To indicate that freshness, or a new lick of paint as Powell described it, an area was wiped clean on each print. This outer stroke led Jimmy to request that the inner bag be prepared in such a way that it would colour when water was applied.

Finally Peter Grant insisted all the sleeves be shrink wrapped into a brown paper bag so that no buyer would know which sleeve he would be receiving, and also to prove that you could stuff a Led Zepp album into a paper bag and it would still sell! And of course it did.

Musically, *In Through The Out Door* is dominated by John Paul Jones. His influence is stronger than ever before. Disappointingly, the album suffers from a less than crystal clear production, and in hindsight, did possess more than its quota of filler material. Still, what's good is very good indeed, and at the time was indication enough to suggest that Led Zeppelin were ready to enter the new decade with as much enthusiasm as they had entered the Seventies.

IN THE EVENING
Jones, Page, Plant

Studios: Polar Music, Stockholm; Plumpton, Sussex

TO ILLUSTRATE the feeling of rebirth, Page pulls out the old violin bow to create a dramatic opening segment (reminiscent of his work on the soundtrack of Kenneth Anger's Lucifer Rising). From there on, this is a very satisfying flexing of the muscles.

Jimmy also used a Gizmatron (an effect invented by Lol Creme and Kevin Godley of 10cc) device to increase distortion and create the slamming door effect heard at the onset of the solo. Plant's arrogant strutting vocal is undercut by a majestic cascading riff that ricochets off every wall. When the whole thing slows up momentarily, some shimmering minor chords and fluid bass take control. Then it's headlong into a powerful fade. A performance that pushed its chest out as if to say... take that. Clearly Led Zeppelin still had... it.

Live performances
Premièred at the Copenhagen

shows, and in for Knebworth where it stood out as a stunning new creation, entering the set for Page's visual violin bow segment. Also used on the Over Europe 1980 tour. Page played the string-bending blue Strat on this track. Plant then revived the number to great effect on his Now And Zen solo tour in 1988. He also performed it with Fairport Convention at their 1992 Cropredy Festival. Revived extensively by Page & Plant on their 1995/6 world tour and on the opening night only in Zagreb on their 1998 world tour.

SOUTH BOUND SUAREZ
Jones, Plant

Studios: Polar Music; Plumpton

WITH ITS rollicking piano intro, this is a track that conjures up the Louisiana/New Orleans bar room feel of the sleeve. Plant's vocals are somewhat strained and overall the only redeeming feature of a rather lack-lustre outing is a measured Page solo and the do-wop fade out.

Live performances
Never performed live.

FOOL IN THE RAIN
Jones, Page, Plant

Studio: Polar Music

DURING THE summer of 1978, the World Cup was played out in Argentina against a variety of samba-inspired TV soccer themes. Those South American themes were still ringing in the ears of Plant and Jones when Led Zeppelin reconvened to plan this album. Thus the idea emerged to layer on their own samba half way through the hop-skip riff arrangement of this tune. Crazy as it sounds, it works beautifully right through J.P.'s street whistles to Bonzo's delightfully constructed timpani crashes. Back at mid-tempo, Jimmy puts in a quite exquisite solo. A most successful alliance that grew out of Plant's insistence that new territory had to be investigated if they were to sustain his own personal commitment, a point thrashed out at their rehearsal sessions at Clearwell Castle in May of 1978. 'Fool In The Rain 'became their sixth US Top 40 hit when it reached number 21 in January 1980.

Live performances
Never performed live.

HOT DOG
Page, Plant

Studio: Polar Music

'HOT DOG' owes much to the state of Texas and to the state of a particular female in Texas. Musically it grew out of their London pre-production rehearsals, where as usual they began by running through old Elvis Presley and Ricky Nelson material from the fifties. A rockabilly country hoedown, it was obviously great fun to record and did develop into a crowd pleaser on the European tour (though it sounded a little mystifying on its Knebworth première). On record though, time has not been too kind to it, and as for that solo... are you putting us on J. Page?

Live performances

Brought in for Copenhagen and Knebworth and retained for all the 1980 Over Europe dates. An official promo video of this track, filmed at Knebworth, was made available by Swan Song to the record industry in America.

CAROUSELAMBRA
Jones, Page, Plant

Studio: Polar Music

THE EPIC. Driven along relentlessly by Jones' keyboard thrusts, 'Carouselambra' is a typically grandiose Zeppelin marathon. It was first conceived in rehearsal at their Clearwell Castle get-together in May 1978. This is one of the only tracks cut in the studio that employs the Gibson double-neck guitar, which can be heard to great effect by Page during the slower middle section.

Lyrically, this is a typically mystical affair made even more obscure by a very muddy mix that all but buries Plant's vocal. Allegedly, it harks back to the past to act as a shroud for a contemporary Plant observation of a person who in his words will one day realise it was written about them and proclaim...

"My God! Was it really like that?"

'Carouselambra' covers a lot of ground during its 10-minute duration, and though the actual recording restricts its majestic quality somewhat, the intentions here remain honourable.

Live performances

Sadly, never played live. They had planned to work on an arrangement of this for Led Zeppelin: The Eighties Campaign. It certainly had the scope to be a compelling live piece. A section of the song was incorporated into 'In The Evening' by Page & Plant on their 1995/6 world tour.

ALL MY LOVE
Jones, Plant

Studios: Polar Music; Plumpton

AS CAN BE observed from the composing credits, this came from an occasion when Plant and Jones arrived at the studio first. A very successful attempt to write a melodic, pretty love song, the lyrics are full of sincerity, inspiring Robert to turn in a superb vocal performance. Jones' classical keyboard solo is another revelation, while Jimmy adds some subtle acoustic picking. 'All My Love' mirrors the reflective and mellow mood Plant found himself in during 1978. That he could still transfer those feelings into the group's music proved to them that collectively Led Zeppelin remained very much in the present tense.

There exists a wonderful,

extended alternative version of 'All My Love'. It clocks in at seven minutes and two seconds and has a complete ending, with Plant echoing his "I get a bit lonely" sentiments in an arrangement that was later employed on the 1980 live version. The original two inch master reel of this outtake as recorded at Polar Studios on November 14, 1978, is labelled 'The Hook', a working title which probably refers to the commercial nature of the song.

Live performances

The only previously untried number inserted into the 'Over Europe' tour in 1980. It became one of the best received performances of the whole tour. Lines from the song were included by Page & Plant within the Calling To You/Whole Lotta Love medleys on their 1995/96 world tour.

I 'M GONNA CRAWL
Jones, Page, Plant

Studios: Polar Music; Plumpton

ENHANCED by yet another major Jones contribution, this time a smooth synthesised string arrangement, 'I'm Gonna Crawl' is a relaxed and confident slow blues. Plant saw this as an attempt to capture the laid-back approach of the mid-Sixties work of Wilson Pickett, O.V. Wright and Otis Redding, Pickett's 'It's Too Late' being a particular reference point. Some forceful Bonham sparring with Page brings a dynamic quality to the track, while Jimmy's solo is his best slow blues performance since the third album. A pleading Plant vocal brings the track to a satisfying finale.

Live performances
Never performed live.

Coda

Swan Song A0051 | UK Album Chart: No 4; US: No 6

DURING 1981 THERE WAS MUCH SPECULATION WITHIN THE INNER SWAN Song sanctum over whether a final album would be delivered. The original Swan Song contract signed with Atlantic in 1974, called for five albums. With no intention of keeping the group together in any form, contractual and business reasons therefore led Page, Plant and Jones to go ahead with a final album project.

The intention was to profile their 12-year career with a collection of quality left-over tracks. Page began shifting through the tapes at his Sol recording studio in Berkshire during the summer of 1981. After completing the *Death Wish II* soundtrack, he called in Robert and J. P. to mix, and in some cases overdub, the eight selected tracks. The album had a working title of

Early Days And Latter Days and was compiled for release early in 1982. Its eventual release was held over until Robert's début solo set *Pictures At Eleven* hit the shops in the summer.

The sleeve involved collating a selection of off-stage group photos to form a centre spread collage. Ideas thrown around at a meeting this author had with Page and Plant in March 1982 to discuss this projected sleeve ranged from using stills from their Knebworth rehearsal video filmed at Bray studios in June 1979, to digging up some celebrated 'road fever' pics from the 1973 US tour. Both of those ideas (in the latter case not surprisingly!) were ultimately vetoed. The final 30 photographs were eventually housed in a grey outer sleeve simply engraved with the words Led Zeppelin and *Coda*, an appropriate revised title, defined in the dictionary as, "An independent passage introduced after the main part of a movement."

Coda was released on November 22, 1982, with little pre-publicity. A low-key advertising campaign employing posters with a symbolic illustration of nine mysterious discs, backed it up. In the UK, only the traditional crop of seasonal TV-advertised titles prevented it reaching the top spot. It entered and stayed at number four. In America *Coda* reached a credible sixth on the *Billboard* chart.

The release of *Coda* neatly tied up the loose recorded ends and it remains an enjoyable and affectionate summary of the Led Zeppelin era – chronicling their studio development during the years 1969 to 1978 – with plenty of previously unheard surprises along the way.

WE'RE GONNA GROOVE
B.B. King

Studios: Bethea Studio: Morgan, London; The Sol, Berkshire

ONE OF the great 'lost' Zepp performances finally receives an official airing. 'We're Gonna Groove' was recorded during a hectic week in June 1969 when their schedule ran as follows:

Saturday gig at Bristol Colston Hall.

Monday radio session for John Peel's *Top Gear* in Bond Street, London.

Wednesday recording session at Morgan studios London.

Thursday gig at Portsmouth Guild Hall.

Friday radio concert for the BBC at the Playhouse Theatre London.

Saturday live appearance at the Bath Festival Of Blues.

Sunday 6pm and 9pm appearances at the Royal Albert Hall Pop Proms, London.

Phew! No time for a two-year lay off in those days. 'We're Gonna Groove' was chosen as their set opener on the UK, Europe and US dates in early 1970, and will have already been familiar to keen Zepp

John Bonham, Robert Plant, Jimmy Page and John Paul Jones outside the Savoy Hotel in London, December 11, 1969, following an awards ceremony.

Presence (April, 1976) and *The Soundtrack From The Song Remains The Same* (October, 1976)

John Bonham

Robert on stage at the Empire Pool, Wembley, November 1971.

In Through The Out Door (August, 1979) and *Coda* (November, 1982)

Jimmy Page at the Swansong offices, July 1979.

Robert Plant on stage in 1977.

Jimmy Page on stage at Knebworth, August 1979.

Plant and Page on stage at Knebworth.

The group on stage during their final tour, 'Over Europe', summer 1980.

Plant, Jones and Page, backstage at the
Philadelphia Live Aid concert, July 13, 1985.

collectors as a live bootleg track. This studio version, deemed unusable for *Led Zeppelin II*, is full of slashing Page guitar (with sub-octivider effects added at The Sol in 1982), great Bonham percussion and typically frantic Plant vocal. The track's full on 1970 potency can now be viewed in the stunning opening Royal Albert Hall segment on the 2003 Led Zeppelin DVD set.

Live performances

The set opener of the UK, European and US dates January to April 1970, it was then discarded in favour of 'Immigrant Song'. Revived by Page & Plant as an insert into the 'Calling To You'/'Whole Lotta Love' medlies on their 1995/96 world tour. Plant also performed the song in it's original arrangement during his *Priory Of Brion* gigs in 1999/2000.

POOR TOM
Page, Plant

Studios: Olympic, London; The Sol

ONE OF THE *Led Zeppelin III* left-overs from the June 1970 sessions at Olympic, 'Poor Tom' is another product of the trip to Bron-Y-Aur. A semi-acoustic bluesy jug-band work-out, it's propelled along by an inventive Bonham shuffle that holds up the momentum all the way through. Plant throws in some harmonica blowing for good measure.

Live performances

Never performed live.

I CAN'T QUIT YOU BABY
Willie Dixon

Studio: Live sound check recording from the Royal Albert Hall, mixed at The Sol

MONDAY, January 9, 1970, is the next dateline revisited. This alleged soundcheck rehearsal run-through of a first album blues standard does, in fact, sound very similar to the actual live version performed in the evening (as captured on film by the crew employed to work on the intended Led Zeppelin documentary). Did the tapes get mislabelled? Well whatever version it is, this a great example of Led Zeppelin, the blues band, having a blow and enjoying every minute of it.

Live performances

Included in the set from 1968 through to the fifth US tour in 1970. Revived as part of the 'Whole Lotta Love' medley for the Japan, UK and Europe dates 1972/3. Also rehearsed at the Atlantic reunion in May 1988. Performed by Page & Plant on their first reunion prior to their MTV *Unledded* filming at the Alexis Korner benefit show at the Buxton Opera House April 17 1994. Occasionally used as an insert within 'Babe I'm Gonna Leave You' by Page & Plant during their 1995/96 shows and as an insert within 'How Many More Times' on their 1998 world tour.

WALTER'S WALK
Page, Plant

Studios: Stargroves, Berkshire, with The Rolling Stones' Mobile; The Sol

A N UNEXPECTED gem. Laid down in May 1972 with Eddie Kramer and left off Houses Of The Holy, 'Walter's Walk' is a tense, un-melodic rocker spearheaded by a solid Page riff. The overall sound here shares little of the crispness of most of the Houses material. Only the drumming brings to mind that particular era. It obviously didn't fit into the game plan of the time, but emerges as a dense and intoxicating outing.

It's quite possible that this song existed only as a basic backing track until the band put *Coda* together. Plant's vocal delivery sounds very Eighties in feel (not unlike 'Burning Down One Side from his first solo album) and it could well be that a new vocal was recorded at The Sol Studios in early 1982.

Live performances
Never performed live in its entirety, the basic structure of 'Walter's Walk' was, however employed during 'Dazed And Confused' on their 1972 Australian and US tour dates as can be heard on the *How The West Was Won* live CD.

OZONE BABY
Page, Plant

Studios: Polar Music, Stockholm; The Sol

I T'S BACK TO November 1978 for an 'Out Door' left-over. 'Ozone Baby' has an affable exuberance spurred on by Plant, who smiles through the whole thing. Up-tempo and friendly, its charm is further enhanced by a fluttering Page solo and some harmonised vocal effects.

Live performances
Never performed live- though elements of the riff can be heard in live arrangements of Dazed And Confused on their 1975 US tour.

DARLENE
Bonham, Jones, Page, Plant

Studios: Polar Music; The Sol

T WO DAYS later in Stockholm we join the boys for a jiving rock-'n'roll jam. 'Darlene' is just that. Starting out as a jerkily riffed, playful exercise with tinkling Jones piano and off beat drumming, it develops into a rousing fade out with Page pulling out some classic James Burton licks.

Live performances
Never performed live.

BONZO'S MONTREUX
Bonham

Studios: Mountain, Montreux; The Sol

THE OFT-TOUTED, total percussion number Bonzo cut with Jimmy during their exile in Montreux in September 1976. Bonzo includes all manner of percussive effects here, aided by Jimmy's electronic treatments. A tuneful pattern does emerge from the soloing, primarily a high pitched steel drum sound created by Page's newly acquired harmoniser. An affectionate if unspectacular tribute, though hardly the best showcase for John Bonham's vast talent.

Live performances
Never performed live.

WEARING AND TEARING
Page, Plant

Studios: Polar Music; The Sol

A FINAL Tuesday rendezvous with Led Zeppelin in the Abba studios. Recorded on November 21, 1978, 'Wearing And Tearing' is the number Page and Plant had threatened would keep up with the punk rock bands in London. It was also the track nearly made available to the 300,000-plus Knebworth audience.

Thankfully it sees the light of day here. This vibrant Plant plea for the right cure takes off at breakneck speed, side-stepping periodically to let Plant *a cappella* the lines *à la* 'Black Dog'. It gets more and more frantic with Page playing at a frightening pace, supported by that ever steady Bonham/Jones rhythm section. The intensity accelerates until the song hots up to an abrupt ending.

Live performances
Never performed live in the Zeppelin era, though it was slated to emerge in the 'Led Zeppelin: The Eighties Campaign'. Twelve years on it was a live vehicle with which Plant and Page would wow the Knebworth 1990 audience. The 1990 live delivery of the final track on the tenth Led Zeppelin album proved yet again the sheer potency of their material when in the hands of the original composers. For a few short minutes the song really did remain the same...

LED ZEPPELIN REMASTERED 1990

Led Zeppelin

Atlantic 7567821441/2/4 (six albums, four CDs, four cassettes)
UK Album Chart: No 48

TRACKS: Whole Lotta Love, Heartbreaker, Communication Breakdown, Babe I'm Gonna Leave You, What Is And What Should Never Be, Thank You, I Can't Quit You Baby, Dazed And Confused, Your Time Is Gonna Come, Ramble On, Travelling Riverside Blues, Friends, Celebration Day, Hey Hey What Can I Do, White Summer/Black Mountain Side, Black Dog, Over The Hills And Far Away, Immigrant Song, The Battle Of Evermore, Bron-Y-Aur Stomp, Tangerine, Going To California, Since I've Been Loving You, D'Yer Mak'er, Gallows Pole, Custard Pie, Misty Mountain Hop, Rock And Roll, The Rain Song, Stairway To Heaven, Kashmir, Trampled Underfoot, For Your Life, No Quarter, Dancing Days, When The Levee Breaks, Achilles Last Stand, The Song Remains The Same, Ten Years Gone, In My Time Of Dying, In The Evening, Candy Store Rock, The Ocean, Ozone Baby, Houses Of The Holy, Wearing And Tearing, Poor Tom, Nobody's Fault But Mine, Fool In The Rain, In The Light, The Wanton Song, Moby Dick-Bonzo's Montreux, I'm Gonna Crawl, All My Love

Remasters

Atlantic Zep 1, 7567804152, 4 (triple album, double CD, double cassette)
UK Album Chart: No 10

TRACKS: 'Communication Breakdown', 'Babe I'm Gonna Leave You', 'Good Times, Bad Times, Dazed And Confused', 'Heartbreaker', 'Whole Lotta Love', 'Ramble On, 'Since I've Been Loving You', 'Celebration Day', 'Immigrant Song, 'Black Dog, 'Rock And Roll', 'Battle Of Evermore', 'Stairway To Heaven', 'The Song Remains The Same', 'D'yer Mak'er', 'No Quarter','Houses Of The Holy', 'Trampled Underfoot', 'Kashmir', 'Nobody's Fault But Mine', 'Achilles Last Stand','All My Love', 'In The Evening' (Cassette and CD versions also include Misty Mountain Hop, The Rain Song)

THE RELEASE OF THESE TWO SEPARATE LED ZEPPELIN RETROSPECTIVE collections in the space of two weeks in October 1990, rounded off a year in which the group's popularity reached heights unparalleled since the mid-Seventies. The excitement that greeted the appearance of the Led Zeppelin Remastered project emphasised how much the group – and the timeless and eclectic quality of their music – had been missed during the 'disposable pop' atmosphere of the Eighties.

The whole exercise was a tremendous success, both critically and commercially. Reviewers who had previously been cold towards Led Zeppelin felt obliged to reconsider their opinions in the light of their influence and the obvious fact that so many of those groups that followed in their wake were noticeably inferior in every department.

And for a boxed set costing almost £50 sales throughout the world were extraordinary. Much of this may have been due to the fact that Led Zeppelin's catalogue had never been shamelessly exploited in the same way that, say, The Who or The Stones' had been. That there had never been a Led Zep *Best Of* compilation before – and the aftermath of its eventual release – was surely a further indication of the astuteness of Peter Grant's long term management strategies as regards quality control.

It had been no secret that Jimmy Page was deeply unhappy with the earliest Led Zeppelin CDs that Atlantic issued without consulting him. Originally produced for vinyl, the music suffered in transit: subtle frequencies in the sound spectrum were lost and the 'ambient' sound that Page had worked so hard to create by the sensitive placement of microphones in the studio was also lost. Small wonder, then, that when Atlantic approached him to remaster the tapes for a compilation collection, he jumped at the idea. Studio time was booked at New York's Sterling studios where Page spent a week in May 1990 with engineer George Marino digitally restoring the bulk of Led Zeppelin's catalogue from the original two-track master tapes.

The plan was to compile a multi-track box set collection for which Page drew up a possible listing for Plant and Jones to sanction. "I really wanted to improve the overall sound spectrum," Page was quoted on the official press release. "Basically it's the same picture with a different frame."

John Paul Jones added: "The songs sound as fresh today as they did when first recorded, and the new positions in the running order seem to put them in a totally different light."

The original compilation concept was to package 54 tracks in a de luxe box with accompanying booklet of photos and essays. Atlantic's European distributors East West also managed to clear a separate edited version of the set for Europe only. This condensed version, virtually a greatest hits package aimed squarely at the lucrative Christmas market, appeared under the title *Remasters* as a 24-track, triple album and 26-track, double CD and cassette on October 15. A full marketing campaign including a TV advertisement was prepared as the Zepp catalogue finally succumbed to the Nineties commercial treatment. Plant, Page and Jones did retain part of their original strategy in vetoing the planned release of 'Stairway To Heaven' as a UK single.

The *Remasters* set was deleted in the UK in the summer of 1991, and since it contains one track not on the box set ('Good Times Bad Times'), it is sure to be a future Zepp vinyl collectable. After a period of withdrawal the set reappeared on catalogue in 1992 on CD and cassette. It was also eventually issued in America as a three-CD set with a bonus *Led Zeppelin Profiled* official interview promo CD. The real gem for Zeppelin enthusiasts was the October 29 appearance of the 54-track box set, simply entitled *Led Zeppelin* and spread over six albums, four CDs and four cassettes.

Despite certain faults – the dearth of selections from *Physical Graffiti*, no chronological live tracks or alternate studio takes, the factual errors in the visually superb accompanying booklet (Live Aid in 1987!) – this set does stand as a lasting testament to the diverse musical styles Led Zeppelin approached from 1968 to 1980. Beautifully packaged with a typically enigmatic design featuring the shadow of an airship over those mysterious cornfield circles (which perhaps suggested that Led Zeppelin were somehow responsible for – or at least knew *something* about – their appearance in the first place), it's wonderful to hear so many tracks all at one sitting. For those very familiar with their catalogue, the new sequencing is also a joy – as 'Heartbreaker' switches instantly to 'Communication Breakdown', 'Over The Hills And Far Away' juxtaposes against 'Immigrant Song' and 'The Song Remains The Same' drifts into 'Ten Years Gone'. Note too, the slightly longer intro to 'Nobody's Fault But Mine' with an extra opening Page guitar riff, and the fact that many timings on the original albums were well out (e.g. 'Kashmir' is now correctly listed as being 8.31 in duration, and not the long presumed 9.41).

And there are some new delights. The little heard Zeppelin III-era 'Hey Hey What Can I Do', previously available only on a long-deleted UK Atlantic sampler album, and as the B-side to the 1970 'Immigrant Song' US, European single, retains all its original summer of 1970 semi-acoustic warmth. It's also great to hear the spiralling blues slide of the BBC *Top Gear* 1969 radio remnant 'Travelling Riverside Blues' – a Page, Plant, Robert Johnson interpretation. Nostalgic memories also prevail on the live BBC take of 'White Summer/Black Mountain Side' from June 27, 1969. Jimmy has also included an affectionate Bonzo tribute, an amalgamation of 'Moby Dick' and 'Bonzo's Montreux', produced with the aid of Synclavier programming at Atlantic's Synclavier suite.

All in all, the overall sound quality is greatly enhanced, with Page adding a new punch and clarity from the original analogue tapes.

The reception the boxed set received exceeded even Atlantic's own high expectations. By the end of 1992 it had shifted over a million units worldwide, making it the best selling historical retrospective package of its kind, an extraordinary testament to Led Zeppelin's ongoing power, influence and popularity.

The previously unreleased material is analysed below.

TRAVELLING RIVERSIDE BLUES
Page, Plant, Robert Johnson

Recorded at the Aeolian Hall, London

ONE OF THE legendary Zepp BBC performances recorded on June 24, 1969, by John Waters at the BBC's Aeolian Hall in Bond Street. This was one of the few BBC tracks on which Page was able to dub extra guitar tracks. An adaptation of an old Robert Johnson tune, it was initially aired on John Peel's *Top Gear* show on Sunday June 28, 1969, under the title 'Travelling Riverside Blues '69'. Its renown in collecting circles is largely due to the fact that it was a special recording intended only for radio broadcast. It was interest from US radio interviewers and fans during his Outrider tour that led him to negotiate with BBC Enterprises for its release on the boxed set. A video promo with out-take footage from *The Song Remains The Same* was cut together for use by MTV and other interested TV outlets.

The track itself is a superb remnant from mid-'69, and remains for me one of their most complete performances, not least for Page's won-derful slide guitar work and Plant's teasing ad-libs ("Ahh why doncha come in my kitchen"). A superbly packaged one track promo CD single was issued for radio play in the US, which resulted in the track reaching number seven on the *Billboard* Top Rock Tracks Top 50 chart in November 1990, culled from national album rock radio air-play reports. In my extensive collection, this promo CD takes pride of place as my favourite CD single of all time.

Live performances
Never performed live.

WHITE SUMMER, BLACK MOUNTAIN SIDE
Page

Recorded live at the London Playhouse Theatre for BBC radio

THIS RECORDING comes from the live broadcast made from the Playhouse Theatre on June 27, 1969, for the pilot programme of Radio One's *In Concert* series. Zeppelin's involvement came about after Jimmy told producer Jeff Griffin that Zeppelin had enjoyed record-ing for *Top Gear* but felt the scope of the session didn't allow them sufficient time to display what the band could achieve. Griffin told Jimmy he was trying to get a one hour concert special off the ground and invited Zep to record the pilot programme. Broadcast on June 27, 1969, it set the seal on the long running In Concert series which began a regular spot the following January.

The '69 In Concert has been much bootlegged and many fans will already be familiar with the 'White Summer'/'Black Mountain Side' segment.

Live performances
It was a staple inclusion of the mid-'69 to early '70 dates, and gives Page an opportunity to indulge in a bit of the old CIA, accompanied on timpani and other assorted percussion by John Bonham.

HEY HEY WHAT CAN I DO
Page, Plant, Jones, Bonham

Studio: Island, London

THIS TRACK has long been a much sought after Zep rarity and its inclusion on the box is most welcome. A product of the easygoing summer of 1970 sessions at Island Studios, having been conceived in rehearsal at Bron-Y-Aur and Headley Grange, it is one of the most relaxed and commercial group compositions of this era, managing to balance the new found mellowness with the familiar dynamics. Note for example how Robert places just the right emphasis on the line "Gotta little woman

and she won't be true", and just when you expect a switch to the cranked up Marshall amps they allow the song to slip back into a warm country flavoured mandolin led melody. The collapsing finale recalls the finish of 'In My Time Of Dying'.

All in all, this deserved a wider platform instead of being tucked away on the B-side to the US single of 'Immigrant Song' and as a token attraction on the obscure 'New Age Of Atlantic' sampler.

Live performances
Never performed live by Zeppelin however Page & Plant did perform the song on the US leg of their 1995 world tour. Performed by Page with The Black Crowes on their 1999 US tour dates. Plant occasionally performed the song with Strange Sensation on their 2002 tour.

MOBY DICK, BONZO'S MONTREUX
Page, Jones, Bonham

Studios: Mirror Sound, Los Angeles, Mayfair, New York, A&R, New York (Moby Dick); Mountain, Montreux, The Sol, Cookham (Bonzo's Montreux)

ALTHOUGH strictly speaking this is not really new or unheard material, the amalgamation is. It came about after Jimmy scanned the lists the others had compiled and found both these titles prominently featured. The idea to combine elements of both tracks came after he'd checked the tempo on a metronome. During the remastering period, Jimmy booked into the Atlantic Synclavier Suite in New York and, with help from John Mahoney, pieced the two tracks together using Synclavier programming. The result is an affectionate blend of two of Bonzo's most illustrious moments.

Boxed Set II

Atlantic 82477; September 1993 | UK chart position: No. 56

TRACKS: 'Good Times Bad Times', 'We're Gonna Groove', 'Night Flight', 'That's The Way', 'Baby Come On Home', 'The Lemon Song', 'You Shook Me', 'Boogie With Stu', 'Bron-Y-Aur', 'Down By The Seaside', 'Out On The Tiles', 'Black Mountain Side', 'Moby Dick', 'Sick Again', 'Hot Dog', 'Carouselambra', 'South Bound Suarez', 'Walter's Walk', 'Darlene', 'Black Country Woman', 'How Many More Times', 'The Rover', 'Four Sticks', 'Hats Off To (Roy) Harper', 'I Can't Quit You Baby', 'Hot's On For Nowhere', 'Livin' Lovin' Maid (She's Just A Woman)', 'Royal Orleans', 'Bonzo's Montreux', 'The Crunge', 'Bring It On Home', 'Tea For One'

DUE TO THE SUCCESS OF THE FIRST *REMASTERS* PROJECT, JIMMY PAGE responded to Atlantic's request that he work on the balance of tracks left off the set in readiness for a second box set release in 1993. After completing the mastering of the Coverdale, Page album at New York's Sterling Studios in the autumn of 1992, Jimmy immediately set to work on the second Remasters set, again working with engineer George Marino.

The plan was to remaster the 31 performances from the Zeppelin catalogue that had been missed off the first compilation, and once again Jimmy gave careful consideration to the sequencing so as to again offer as balanced a presentation as possible. Although most of the more familiar Zeppelin classics found their way on to the first box, this second collection incorporates many lesser acclaimed but equally important stepping stones. From the gentle acoustic beauty of 'That's The Way' and 'Bron-Y-Aur', through lengthy epics like 'How Many More Times' and 'Carouselambra' to off-the-wall nuggets like 'Walter's Walk' and 'Night Flight', the breadth of diversity is again quite startling and makes *Boxed Set II* a hugely enjoyable companion to the earlier collection.

Boxed Set II contains just one previously unissued track 'Baby Come On Home'...

BABY COME ON HOME
Page, Plant

Studio: Olympic, London

THIS TRACK stems from an old master reel marked 'Yardbirds, October 10, 1968,' a clear reference to its vintage as being the period when the name Led Zeppelin was still under consideration. The master tape went mysteriously missing for a number of years and allegedly turned up in a refuse bin outside Olympic Studios in 1991.

On the original session the engineer dubs the track 'Tribute To Bert Berns', a reference to the Sixties manager, producer, writer who wrote 'Twist And Shout' and 'Hang On Sloopy' and produced Van Morrison and Them amongst others. The original master tape of this first album outtake was dusted down and mixed by Mike Fraser, the co-producer of the Coverdale, Page album. Appearing now under the title 'Baby Come On Home', it's a welcome bonus, a slow blues tune and possibly Robert's idea carried over from The Band Of Joy. It's very commercial, with backing vocals on the chorus, Jones on Hammond organ and Jimmy confined to some low key Leslied guitar runs.

It's not hard to see why it didn't fit into the more energetic feel of the rest of the first album and perhaps it was under consideration as an early single as it would have sat nicely alongside the '68 blues boom period releases from Fleetwood Mac, Chicken Shack and the like.

Live performances
Never performed live.

OTHER COMPILATIONS & LIVE RECORDINGS

The Complete Studio Recordings

Atlantic: 7-82526-2 | September 1993

WITH ALL OFFICIALLY AVAILABLE LED ZEPPELIN TRACKS NOW REMASTERED, Atlantic issued a de luxe box set package containing all the original ten studio albums on CD. The version of the *Coda* album includes the bonus tracks to be found on the earlier boxed sets, specifically 'Baby Come On Home' (1968 outtake previously issued on Boxed Set 2), 'Travelling Riverside Blues'/'White Summer – Black Mountain Side' (BBC session recordings previously issued on the 1990 Led Zeppelin box set) and 'Hey Hey What Can I Do' (1970 outtake previously issued on the 1990 Led Zeppelin box set)

Early Days

The Best Of Led Zeppelin Volume One

Atlantic: 7567-83268-2; November 1999 | UK Album Chart: No.55

TRACKS: 'Good Times Bad Times', 'Babe I'm Gonna Leave You', 'Dazed And Confused', 'Communication Breakdown', 'Whole Lotta Love', 'What Is And What Should Never Be', 'Immigrant Song', 'Since I've Been Loving You', 'Black Dog', 'Rock And Roll', 'The Battle Of Evermore', 'When The Levee Breaks', 'Stairway To Heaven'

THE FIRST OF A NEW TWO-VOLUME CHRONOLOGICAL 'BEST OF' PACKAGE. This includes an enhanced CD video version of 'Communication Breakdown' sourced from a mimed appearance the band made on a Swedish TV show in March 1969.

The sleeve design depicting the group members superimposed into Apollo space suits was sourced from a poster featured in a French magazine in the early Seventies.

Latter Days

The Best Of Led Zeppelin Volume Two

Atlantic: 7567-83278-2; April 2000 | UK Album Chart: No 40

TRACKS: 'The Song Remains The Same', 'No Quarter', 'Houses Of The Holy', 'Trampled Underfoot', 'Kashmir', 'Ten Years Gone', 'Achilles Last Stand', 'Nobody's Fault But Mine', 'All My Love', 'In The Evening'

THE SECOND OF THE NEW 'BEST OF' VOLUMES, THIS ONE CONCENTRATING ON the years 1973 to 1979. This package includes an enhanced CD video version of 'Kashmir', featuring the studio version of the track synched to previously unseen footage of their 1975 Earls Court shows.

The Very Best Of Led Zeppelin

Early Days And Latter Days

Atlantic: 75678-36195; February 2003 | UK Album Charts: No 11

TRACKS: 'Good Times Bad Times', 'Babe I'm Gonna Leave You', 'Dazed And Confused', 'Communication Breakdown', 'Whole Lotta Love', 'What Is And What Should Never Be', 'Immigrant Song', 'Since I've Been Loving You', 'Black Dog', 'Rock And Roll', 'The Battle Of Evermore', 'When The Levee Breaks', 'Stairway To Heaven', 'The Song Remains The Same', 'No Quarter', 'Houses Of The Holy', 'Trampled Underfoot', 'Kashmir', 'Ten Years Gone', 'Achilles Last Stand', 'Nobody's Fault But Mine', 'All My Love', 'In The Evening' (includes enhanced CD video of 'Communication Breakdown' and 'Kashmir')

A STRAIGHT REPACKAGE OF THE TWO VOLUMES LISTED ABOVE IN AN OUTER slip case. Aided by a TV advertising campaign and the interest spurred by the DVD and *How The West Was Won* live album, this set took Zeppelin back into the top 20 album chart for the first time since 1990.

BBC Sessions

Atlantic: 7567-83061-2; November 1997 | UK Album Charts: No 23

TRACKS: 'You Shook Me', 'I Can't Quit You Baby', 'Communication Breakdown', 'Dazed And Confused', 'The Girl I Love She Got Long Black Wavy Hair', 'What Is And What Should Never Be', 'Communication Breakdown', 'Travelling Riverside Blues', 'Whole Lotta Love', 'Somethin' Else', 'Communication Breakdown', 'I Can't Quit You Baby', 'You Shook Me', 'How Many More Times', 'Immigrant Song', 'Heartbreaker', 'Since I've Been Loving You', 'Black Dog', 'Dazed And Confused', 'Stairway To Heaven', 'Going To California', 'That's The Way', 'Whole Lotta Love (medley) 'Boogie Chillun'/ 'Fixin' To Die'/'That's Alright Mama'/'A Mess Of Blues', 'Thank You'

L ONG SINCE THE SOURCE OF COUNTLESS ZEPPELIN BOOTLEGS, THE GROUP'S 1969 and 1971 BBC radio sessions were finally given an official overhaul by Jimmy Page in 1997. Working with mastering engineer Jon Astley, Page edited the sessions into a cohesive double CD set that serves to illustrate Zeppelin's rapid musical development during their early years together.

Disc One draws on the four 1969 radios sessions: studio recorded sets from March 23 and June 29 broadcasts for John Peel's *Top Gear*, a June 22 broadcast for Chris Grant's *Tasty Pop Sundae* and a live broadcast from the Playhouse Theatre on June 27, recorded as a pilot for what would emerge as the long running Radio One *In Concert* series. This live recording was subsequently aired under the title *One Night Stand* on August 10.

Throughout the disc, Page cleverly employs differing versions of the same songs: three versions of 'Communication Breakdown' and two apiece of 'You Shook Me' and 'I Can't Quite You Baby'. Each contains subtle differences illustrating Zep's forte to constantly expand and improvise their songs in a live setting. The latter pair of Willie Dixon numbers also illustrate how they took traditional blues styles and turned them into something loud and primal. On the March 23 version of 'Dazed And Confused' their ability to build tension is evident on every wail of Page's wah-wah guitar.

The June 29 *Top Gear* session features embryonic versions of 'Whole Lotta Love' and 'What Is And What Should Never Be' a clear four months before their appearance on *Led Zeppelin II*.

There are also two performances of songs that never graced a Zeppelin album, both drawn from the Chris Grant session. These are a rousing version of 'Something Else', the Eddie Cochran song, and 'The Girl I Love She Got Long Black Wavy Hair', a spontaneous rocker combining elements of the Sleepy John Estes song of the same name and a riff similar to the *Zep II* Bonham showcase 'Moby Dick'.

Disc Two draws on the Radio One *In Concert* broadcast recorded at the Paris Cinema London on April 1, 1971, and aired originally on April 4. At the time the band had just completed a 13-date back to the clubs tour which had taken its toll on Plant's voice This resulted in the postponement of the original *In Concert* date initially set for March 25. By Page's own admission, it was not a magic night but there is still much to enjoy.

At the time the band were breaking in new material from their just recorded fourth album, which would eventually be released the following November.

This BBC show finds then running through a tentative, nervous first radio airing of the fabled 'Stairway To Heaven', a lovely 'Going To California' and a strident 'Black Dog', the later held back from the actual broadcast. The opening bombast of 'Immigrant Song' and 'Heartbreaker' recall the intensity of their on stage prowess of the time. The near 14-minute edit of the 'Whole Lotta Love' medley includes delightful romps through 'Boogie Chillun', 'That's Alright' and 'A Mess Of Blues'. The final bonus is an emotive (and again previously untransmitted) encore of 'Thank You'. Despite the minimal chat between songs, the '71 show retains a strong live atmosphere and is an accurate portrayal of the band as they began to extend their sets ready for the mega stadium gigs to come.

Overall, the official sanctioning of these BBC Sessions provides much needed aural evidence of how the band were developing in those formative years. It stands as an important milestone in their catalogue.

How The West Was Won

Atlantic: 7567-8-3587-2 ; May 2003 | UK Album Chart: No 5; US No 1

TRACKS: 'LA Drone', 'Immigrant Song', 'Heartbreaker', 'Black Dog', 'Over The Hills And Far Away', 'Since I've Been Loving You', 'Stairway To Heaven', 'Going To California', 'That's The Way', 'Bron yr Aur Stomp', 'Dazed And Confused', 'What Is And What Should Never Be', 'Dancing Days', 'Moby Dick', 'Whole Lotta Love', 'Rock And Roll', 'The Ocean', 'Bring It On Home'

WHILST RESEARCHING THE DVD PROJECT PAGE CAME ACROSS THE TAPES OF two complete shows recorded at the LA Forum on June 25 and Long Beach Arena June 27 on their American tour of 1972. Both these dates were well known to ardent Zep collectors. The LA gig had been held in high esteem via an excellent audience recording released on a bootleg CD set titled *Burn Like A Candle*. Three soundboard extracts from the Long Beach gig – 'What Is And What Should Never Be', 'Dancing Days' and 'Moby Dick' – had seeped out on bootleg, giving rise to rumours of the existence of the full tapes.

Together with engineer Kevin Shirley, Page edited the two shows to form a three CD set that finally captures the real deal of Zeppelin live. It's quite breathtaking to hear how far the band had developed barely a year on from the BBC 1971 *In Concert* show. They were simply on fire that summer of '72, brimming with confidence and a knowing arrogance that they had elevated to new heights of onstage telepathy. The set features three previews from the their forthcoming fifth album, *Houses Of The Holy*, which would eventually emerge nine months later. The assured deliveries of 'Over The Hills And Far Away', 'Dancing Days' and 'The Ocean' are typical of the wave of optimism they were rolling on. An experimental, marathon-length 'Dazed And Confused' includes spin off improvisations on 'The Crunge', another *Houses* preview, plus the newly recorded backing track 'Walters Walk' which would not see the light of day until the posthumous *Coda* album. The version of 'Stairway To Heaven' features an elongated Page solo and the three track acoustic segment – 'Going To California', 'That's The Way' and 'Bron Yr Aur Stomp' – offers further evidence of their growing acoustic maturity. CD 3 is an absolute tour de force with covers of 'Let's Have A Party', 'Hello Mary Lou' and 'Going Down Slow' within the 'Whole Lotta Love' medley, a storm through 'Rock And Roll', the full on riff power of 'The Ocean' and a rare (for the time) outing for 'Bring It On Home'.

The release of *How The West Was Won* in the spring of 2003 conclusively redressed the lack of a fully representative official live Zeppelin album. The fact that it entered the *Billboard* US chart at number one was a fitting testament to Zeppelin's longevity. And don't rule out further archive releases in the future – a companion set possibly titled *How The East Was Won* sourced from Zep's Japanese tour in 1971 has been rumoured to be under consideration.

THE LED ZEPPELIN DVD

Warner Music Vision 0349 701982; May 2003 | UK Video Chart: No 1

DISC 1: 'We're Gonna Groove', 'I Can't Quite You Baby', 'Dazed And Confused', 'White Summer', 'What Is And What Should Never Be', 'How Many More Times', 'Moby Dick', 'Whole Lotta Love', 'Communication Breakdown', 'C'mon Everybody', 'Something Else', 'Bring It On Home', Extras: Communication Breakdown promo, Danmarks Radio, *Supershow*, *Tous En Scene*

DISC 2: 'Immigrant Song', 'Black Dog', 'Misty Mountain Hop', 'Since I've Been Loving You', 'The Ocean', 'Going To California', 'That's The Way', 'Bron Yr Aur Stomp', 'In My Time Of Dying', 'Trampled Underfoot', 'Stairway To Heaven', 'Rock And Roll', 'Nobody's Fault But Mine', 'Sick Again', 'Achilles Last Stand', 'In The Evening', 'Kashmir', 'Whole Lotta Love', Extras: NYC Press Conference, Down Under, *The Old Grey Whistle Test*, Promos

THIS DVD WAS THE ABSOLUTE GEM AMONGST THE EMBARRASSMENT OF riches Page unleashed on Zeppelin fans in 2003. Four and a half hours of visual footage across two DVDs lovingly restored with 5.1 sound quality. Working with noted video director Dick Carruthers, Page spent over a year tracing and restoring the footage that makes up the simply titled DVD.

Disc 1 features their celebrated Royal Albert Hall show from January 9 1970. This is a vintage portrayal of the band without the visual flash that would occur in later years. Amongst the denim, plimsolls and long flowing hair there are some devastating performances. From Page's laid back swoops and glides on 'I Can't Quite You Baby', through a menacing 'Dazed And Confused', great spirited encore versions of Eddie Cochran's 'C'mon Everybody' and 'Something Else' to a crunching 'Whole Lotta Love'.

Disc 2 opens with a ferocious 'Immigrant Song' sourced from the Long Beach Arena show in 1972 cut to silent Super-8 cine film of the band on stage in Australia that year. The quality and editing of the Madison Square Garden material from 1973 is an absolute revelation, its highlight a rampant 'The Ocean'. It then all fades to the band on stage at Earl's Court. In stark contrast to the exuberance of the Garden, we see Jones, Plant and Page relaxed and front of stage for the acoustic 'Going To California', the very epitome of the light and shade element they strived for. Earl's Court is Zeppelin at their most extravagant as they bulldoze through a permanently on the edge 'In My Time Of Dying', a relentless 'Trampled Underfoot' and a suitably regal 'Stairway To Heaven'. Four years later we see them come out to face the post-punk era in front of tens and thousands at Knebworth – Page's less flamboyant attire is a brave attempt to appear more new wave than old.

Brilliantly edited, the Knebworth footage of 'Kashmir' and 'Achilles Last Stand' is evidence that they were still capable of moments of grandiose majesty. The stunning romp through 'Rock And Roll' is proof enough that despite the lay offs their spirit was still very willing.

A host of additional extras include extracts from the bands 1969 Danish TV and *Supershow* movie appearances, eerie black and white footage from their trip to Iceland in 1970 and bootleg cine film from their 1975 and 1977 US tours.

Alongside the *How the West Was Won* live CD, this monumental two DVD set offers essential insight into what made the group such a force and why their influence still casts a giant shadow. Watching and hearing it all prompts fresh re-evaluation of the band's entire standing.

DVD is the long awaited visual feast that confirms Led Zeppelin's legendary status.

CHRONOLOGY
1944-1980

1944

January 9 James Patrick Page born in Heston, Middlesex.

1946

January 3 John Paul Jones (Baldwin) born in Sidcup, Kent.

1948

May 31 John Henry Bonham born in Redditch, Worcestershire.

August 20 Robert Anthony Plant born in West Bromwich, Staffordshire.

1962

Jimmy Page joins Neil Christian & The Crusaders.

1963

January Jimmy Page's first appearance on record, a session for Jet Harris & Tony Meehan's 'Diamonds'.

October Jimmy Page plays on Carter Lewis & The Southerners' 'Your Mamma's Out Of Town' and gigs with them on some radio dates. John Paul Jones joins Jet Harris & Tony Meehan's backing group.

1964

April John Paul Jones releases a solo single – 'Baja'/'A Foggy Day In Vietnam'. Jones makes his name as one of London's top session arrangers and Jimmy Page establishes himself as one of the top UK session guitarists, playing on countless hit records of the era. Robert Plant plays in his first groups – Andy Long & The Original Jaymen, The Black Snake Moan and The Crawling King Snakes. John Bonham plays in his first groups – Terry Webb & The Spiders and A Way Of Life.

1965

February Jimmy Page releases a solo single – 'She Just Satisfies'/'Keep Moving'.

1966

June Jimmy Page joins The Yardbirds, initially on bass but soon switches to dual lead guitar with Jeff Beck.

October Robert Plant sings lead vocal on Listen's single 'You Better Run'/'Everybody's Gonna Say'.

November Page takes over as lead Yardbirds guitarist following Beck's departure.

December John Paul Jones arranges the strings on The Yardbirds' recording of 'Little Games' at Olympic studios.

1967

Robert Plant links up with John Bonham in The Band Of Joy.

March Release of Robert Plant's solo single 'Our Song' / 'Laughing, Crying, Laughing'. Release of Jeff Beck's 'Hi Ho Silver Lining' single which has the Page composition 'Beck's Bolero' on the B-side. It was while playing on this session that Page heard Keith Moon suggest the name Lead Zeppelin as a possibility for the group they had discussed forming.

August The Yardbirds 'Little Games' album issued in the US. It includes the future Page stage showcase number 'White Summer'.

September Release of Robert Plant's solo single 'Long Time Coming' / 'I've Got A Secret'.

1968

January Band Of Joy play regular London dates at the Middle Earth.

March New Page/Yardbirds track 'I'm Confused' (later to be re-titled 'Dazed And Confused') aired at a session on John Peel's *Top Gear* radio show.

April John Paul Jones performs with Jimmy on a session for Donovan's 'Hurdy Gurdy Man', and asks to be considered for a new group Jimmy is rumoured to be forming.

May Band Of Joy split. Robert records demos at Marquee studios. John Bonham tours with Tim Rose.

May 2 Last Yardbirds recording session at CBS studios in New York includes Page's 'Tangerine'.

June 5 Last Yardbirds US gig in Alabama.

June 22 Announced that Keith Relf and Jim McCarty are leaving The Yardbirds.

June Robert Plant gigs and records with Alexis Korner. Jimmy Page records with Joe Cocker at Olympic Studios.

July 7 Final Yardbirds gig at Luton Technical College.

August Jimmy Page, Chris Dreja and former Yardbirds manager Peter Grant see Robert Plant play with Hobstweedle at a Birmingham teacher training college. At this point B.J. Wilson from Procol Harum, who Page had worked with on the Joe Cocker session, and the unknown Paul Francis were being touted as possibles for the vacant drum position. Plant is offered vocalist job in the new Yardbirds line-up after visiting Page's Pangbourne home. Chris Dreja decides not to carry on as bassist in The New Yardbirds. Page calls in John Paul Jones. John Bonham completes the new Yardbirds line-up on Plant's recommendation. First Page, Plant, Jones and Bonham rehearsals, in Gerrard Street, London.

September 7 Existing Yardbirds dates fulfiled on a Scandinavian tour commencing in Copenhagen.

Late September Agreed that The Yardbirds name will be phased out. After considering names such The Mad Dogs, The Mad Boys and The Whoopee Cushions, Page and manager Peter Grant return to Keith Moon's Lead Zeppelin phrase, knocking out the 'a' to simplify the name for American audiences. The New Yardbirds become Led Zeppelin.

October First album recorded at Olympic studios.

October 17 First gig billed as Led Zeppelin at Surrey University.

October 18 Play the Marquee still billed as The Yardbirds.

October 19 Last ever gig billed as The Yardbirds at Liverpool University.

October 25 Debut as Led Zeppelin at Surrey University

November 9 Plant marries Maureen in London. The 'reception' is Led Zeppelin's first billed London show at the Roundhouse, Chalk Farm.

November Grant clinches worldwide deal with Atlantic and forms Superhype publishing company.

December Month of UK club gigs.

December 26 Commence first American tour at the Auditorium in Denver, Colorado.

1969

January 17 *Led Zeppelin* album issued in America.

February 15 First US tour ends at Three Image club Miami.

February Led Zeppelin's first album enters *Billboard* Top 40.

March More club dates in the UK.

March 17 Scandinavian tour includes 30-minute showcase on Danish TV (finally aired in the UK 20 years later!).

March 21 Only live UK TV appearance playing 'Communication Breakdown' on BBC2's *How Late It Is.*

March 23 First radio session aired on John Peel's *Top Gear*.

March 25 Filming session at Staines for *Supershow* movie.

March 28 *Led Zeppelin* début album issued in UK.

April More UK gigs, followed by second US visit (first as headliners).

May US tour continues. Début album enters *Billboard* Top 10. Recording sessions commence along the way for the second album.

June 16, 24 Record sessions for BBC Radio One, at Aeolian Hall, London and Maida Vale.

June 13 First proper UK tour commences at Birmingham Town Hall.

June More sessions for second album at Morgan studios.

June 27 Playhouse Theatre London show taped for BBC radio's *In Concert*.

June 28 Appearance at the Bath Festival.

June 29 Two shows at London's Royal Albert Hall Pop Proms.

July 5 Third US tour. Over 20 dates including open air festivals (they miss out on a scheduled appearance at Woodstock). More recording takes place for the second album.

August 31 Third US tour ends at the Texas International Festival in Dallas.

September Short holiday break. Second album is completed.

October 12 Resume touring with selected European dates followed by this Sunday night showcase at London's Lyceum ballroom.

October 17 Led Zeppelin become first rock act to play New York's

Carnegie Hall when they open their fourth US tour.

October 31 Led Zeppelin II released to massive, worldwide sales.

November 8 Fourth US tour ends at San Francisco's Winterland ballroom.

November Initial recording for the third album commences at Olympic. 'Since I've Been Loving You' is tried out as well as 'Jennings Farm Blues'.

December 5 Projected UK release of 'Whole Lotta Love' as an edited single halted by Peter Grant.

December 11 Led Zeppelin's worldwide record sales recognised with a presentation of gold and platinum discs by the Parliamentary secretary to the Board Of Trade at London's Savoy hotel.

1970

January 7 Seven-date UK tour opens in Birmingham.

January 9 Royal Albert Hall gig filmed and recorded for an intended Zeppelin-financed TV documentary. Turned down an offer to appear on the Tom Jones TV show.

January 'Whole Lotta Love' reaches number four on the Billboard chart.

February Edinburgh gig cancelled after Plant receives facial injuries in a car accident. Rescheduled for Feb 17 prior to a trip to Europe.

February 21 European tour kicks off in Helsinki

February 28 K.B Hallen Copenhagen – the group are billed as The Nobs after threat of legal action from Count Von Zeppelin!

March 12 European tour ends in Dusseldorf

March 21 Fifth American tour commences in Vancouver.

April 6 While in Memphis, Led Zeppelin made honorary citizens.

April 17 US tour ends in Arizona.

April 26 Jimmy Page's solo appearance on the Julie Felix BBC 2 aired - he performs a solo version of White Summer/Black Mountain Side.

May Plant and Page write and prepare material for the third album at a remote cottage in Wales called Bron-Y-Aur. Later in the month the group begin recording at Headley Grange in Hampshire.

June Recording sessions at Olympic.

June 22 Reykjavik, Iceland.

June 28 Bill-topping appearance at the Bath Festival.

July 16 Commence short German tour in Cologne

July, early August Commence additional recording for the third album, this time at the newly opened Island Studios.

August 5 Sixth American tour commences in New Haven

August 17 While in Memphis, Page completes mixing of the third album at Ardent studios.

September 19 Final 1970 concerts at Madison Square Garden, New York.

September 27 Back in the UK, Led Zeppelin end The Beatles' reign as Top Group in Melody Maker's annual readers' poll.

October 16 Led Zeppelin honoured with another presentation of gold discs by Parliamentary Secretary to the Board Of Trade, Anthony Grant, recognising their "substantial contribution to the country's healthy balance of exports".

October 23 *Led Zeppelin III* released.

November, December Holiday break and initial fourth album sessions at Island Studios.

1971

January Led Zeppelin take The Rolling Stones' mobile studio to record their fourth album at Headley Grange.

February Overdub sessions at Island studios. Page travels to Los Angeles to mix the tapes at Sunset Sound studios.

February 14 All the group attend the *Disc and Music Echo* awards in London when they are voted the world's top band.

March 5 Back on the road for a British tour commencing at Belfast Ulster Hall. 'Stairway To Heaven' is played live for the first time.

March 23 The UK tour sees them returning to the club venues that first gave them a gig, and ends nostalgically at London's Marquee.

April 4 First broadcast of the much bootlegged BBC Sunday repeated on Wednesday *In Concert* radio show taped the previous month at London's Paris Theatre. Eventually officially released as a part of the BBC Sessions CD set in 1997.

May, June European tour dates.

July 5 Final European tour date ends with a curtailed show at Milan's Vigorelli Stadium due to a riot.

July Fourth album mixed again in London.

August 19 After two warm-up dates in Montreux, their seventh US tour commences in Vancouver.

September 16, 17 US tour ends with two shows in Honolulu, after which the group holiday in Hawaii.

September 23 Five-date Japanese tour commences in Tokyo.

October Led Zeppelin travel back to the UK. Plant and Page visit Thailand, India and Hong Kong.

November 11 UK tour commences at Newcastle-upon-Tyne City Hall.

November 12 𝍄 𝍖 𝍗 𝍘 album issued.

November 20, 21 Two, five-hour Electric Magic appearances at Wembley Empire Pool, with Bronco, Home, and Stone The Crows.

December 7 UK tour ends in Salisbury.

1972

February A planned date in Singapore cancelled when the group is refused entry to the country because of their long hair.

February 16 10-date Australian tour begins in Perth. On the route back, Page and Plant make some experimental recordings in Bombay with the Bombay Symphony Orchestra.

April, May Fifth album recording sessions on location at Stargroves and Olympic studios.

June 6 Eighth American tour opens at the Cobo Hall, Detroit.

June Mixing and recording sessions at Electric Lady studios for the fifth album.

June 28 US tour ends at the Tucson Community Centre.

August, September Holiday break.

October 2 Second Japanese tour commences in Tokyo.

October 28, 29 Two dates at Montreux Casino.

November Fifth album mixed and completed. Announcement of longest ever UK tour prompts 100,000 ticket sales in one day.

November 30 UK tour commences at Newcastle-upon-Tyne City Hall.

December 22, 23 Two Christmas dates at London's Alexandra Palace.

1973

January 2 Plant and Bonham only just make date at Sheffield City Hall after their Bentley breaks down. Plant goes down with 'flu and the following dates at Bradford and Preston have to be rescheduled.

January 30 UK tour ends in Preston.

February 16 Provisional release date of the fifth album to be titled *Houses Of The Holy* not fulfiled due to sleeve problems.

March 2 European tour opens in Copenhagen.

March 26 *Houses Of The Holy* finally released.

April 1, 2 European tour closes with two nights at the Palais de Sport, Paris.

April Led Zeppelin rehearse a new stage rig at the Old Town studios in preparation for a mammoth two-legged US tour.

May 4 Ninth US tour opens to 49,000 fans at the Atlanta Braves Stadium.

May 5 An astounding 56,800 attend Led Zeppelin's second show

of the tour at Tampa Stadium. This sets a record for the largest attendance for a one-act performance, previously held by The Beatles for their Shea Stadium show in 1965.

June 3 First leg of US tour ends with a rescheduled gig at the LA Forum due to Page spraining his finger.

June Mid-tour holiday in Hawaii.

July 6 US tour second leg kicks off in Chicago.

July 23 Film maker Joe Massot begins shooting footage at the request of Peter Grant and the group in Baltimore.

July 24 More screen test footage taken at the Three Rivers Stadium in Pittsburgh.

July 27, 28, 29 Final nights of the US tour at Madison Square Garden recorded and filmed for their movie project. Just before the last show, the theft from a deposit box of $203,000 of the group's money at the Drake Hotel is discovered. The crime goes unsolved.

August 1 Led Zeppelin and entourage return to England for a well earned break. Robert holidays in South Morocco.

August 11 Led Zeppelin offer a reward of $10,000 for the recovery of the money stolen from the Drake Hotel.

September Robert picks up his award for Top Male Singer at the *Melody Maker* Poll Awards lunch in London.

October Joe Massot commences filming individual sequences at the homes of Plant, Page, Jones, Bonham and Peter Grant.

November Initial sixth album sessions at Headley Grange. Bonzo and Jimmy record an Eastern flavoured demo instrumental, later to take shape as 'Kashmir'. Sessions break up when Jones takes a rest to think over his intention to quit the group and become choirmaster at Winchester Cathedral.

December John Paul Jones promotes Madeline Bell's 'Comin' Atcha' album (which he produced) by playing bass on her BBC2 appearance on *Colour My Soul*.

December 10 and 11 Joe Massot and crew film Jimmy's mountain climbing sequence for the movie at Loch Ness.

1974

January In re-signing with Atlantic, Peter Grant announces that all future Led Zeppelin recordings will appear on their own label. The label will also be signing other acts.

January A group party at the Portman Hotel, London, results in a £1,000 bill.

January, February Sixth album sessions resume at Headley Grange with a revitalised John Paul Jones back at the helm.

January Slut Records rumoured to be the title of the new Zeppelin label.

February 14 Jimmy joins Roy Harper on stage at the Rainbow London. Plant and Bonham are also in attendance.

March, April More recording sessions. Their record label, now officially named Swan Song, sets up offices in New York and London and signs Bad Company and Maggie Bell for the US.

May 7 Swan Song Records launched with all members in attendance at two receptions in New York and Los Angeles. During these celebrations the group attend Elvis Presley's LA Forum concert and gain an audience with him after the show.

May On their return, Peter Grant considers offers for the group to headline a one-day festival on July 20 at Knebworth and an August 29 date at the Munich Festival due to be relayed live to 10,000 theatres in America. Both are turned down due to the band's commitments to completing their album and 1973 concert film.

July Mixing sessions at Olympic for the sixth album. This will now be a double set, employing tracks unused from previous albums.

July New director for their film, Peter Clifton, works with the group at Shepperton studios.

August 31 John Paul Jones forms the backing band with Dave Gilmour and Steve Broughton for Roy Harper's free Hyde Park appearance.

September 1, 4 Jimmy Page jams with Bad Company in Austin, Texas, and Central Park, New York. Bad Company's début album will later this month provide Swan Song with its first number one.

September 14 All the group attend the Crosby, Stills, Nash and Young Wembley Stadium show. Page and Bonzo jam with Stills, Young and Nash at an after-show party in Piccadilly.

October 31 Swan Song officially launched with a bizarre party at Chislehurst Caves. All the group attend, plus many guests including Bad Company and first UK signings The Pretty Things.

November 6 The Pretty Things inaugurate Swan Song in the UK with their single 'Is It Only Love'. Announcement of the planned release of Led Zeppelin's new double album *Physical Graffiti* (stated as November 29) and their US tour scheduled to open in January 1975.

November 26 Led Zeppelin gather at the Livewire Theatre in Ealing to begin rehearsals for their US tour.

December 21 Jimmy and Jones jam with Bad Company at their Rainbow gig in London.

1975

January 11, 12 Warm-up dates in Rotterdam and Brussels. Plant records an interview with Bob Harris backstage in Brussels, later shown on *The Old Grey Whistle Test*.

January 17 The group rehearse a revised set in Minneapolis due to Jimmy breaking his finger days before at Victoria station.

January 18 10th US tour opens at the Metro Sports Centre, Minneapolis.

February 3 At the first of three Madison Square Garden shows, Page restores 'Dazed And Confused' to the set for the first time, his injured finger having forced its temporary deletion up until then.

February 14 First leg of the tour completed with a show at the Long Island Coliseum. Plant and Page holiday on the island of Dominica.

February 24 *Physical Graffiti* finally issued worldwide to phenomenal sales.

March 15 Tickets for Led Zeppelin's just-announced Earls Court shows sell out within four hours.

March 27 Final night of the US tour at the Los Angeles Forum.

April Jimmy, Robert and Peter Grant fly to New York on Swan Song business. Jimmy does some mixing on their film soundtrack at Electric Lady studios.

April 19 Two extra dates are added at Earls Court due to what promoter Mel Bush describes as "Unprecedented demand in the history of rock music."

May 10 Swan Song distribute 5,000 copies of a special limited edition UK single coupling 'Trampled Underfoot' with 'Black Country Woman'.

May 17, 18, 23, 24, 25 85,000 people attend Led Zeppelin's five massive shows at the Earls Court arena in London.

May 25 All the group attend an after-show party held at the Swan Song, Earls Court restaurant.

May 26 Robert Plant and wife Maureen leave for a holiday in Agadir. These travels would later be chronicled in the lyrics of 'Achilles Last Stand'.

June Robert meets with Jimmy in Marrakech for the Moroccan folk festival.

June Peter Clifton announces the near completion of the Led Zeppelin feature film.

July Plant and Page continue their travels back through Casablanca and Tangiers, eventually meeting up with the rest of the group at the Montreux Festival. A second US tour is announced for August. This is the start of a year of non-residency for the group for tax purposes. Page and Plant resume their holidays with their families in Rhodes.

August 3 Page leaves for Italy, planning to reunite with the group for rehearsals five days later in Paris.

August 4 Robert and Maureen Plant seriously injured when their rented car goes off the road in Rhodes. Both are air-lifted back to the UK. Plant is forced to recuperate in Jersey due to his tax situation.

September With the upcoming tour plans cancelled, Plant moves to Malibu. Jimmy Page follows. Songwriting commences for a new album in lieu of the tour.

September 14 Plant, Page and Grant attend the 'Renaissance Pleasure Fair' in Novato.

September 27 Page and Bonzo pick up the group's seven *Melody Maker* poll awards at a reception in London.

October Rehearsals held at SIR studios in Hollywood for the recording of a new album.

November Led Zeppelin record their seventh album at Munich's Musicland studios in a mere 18 days.

December 10 Back in Jersey, the group make a surprise appearance at the Beehan, a West Park night club.

December 24 All the group back in England for Christmas.

1976

January 1 In Paris, Plant takes his first unaided steps since the accident.

January In New York Robert holds a round of interviews. Page continues mixing the soundtrack at Electric Lady. Bonzo proclaims on stage at the end of Deep Purple's Radio City Hall show, "Hi, I'm John Bonham from Led Zeppelin and we've got a new album coming out soon!"

February Zeppelin sweep the board in the *NME* readers' poll.

March Back in London, Page holds a series of interviews at the Swan Song office.

April 5 The seventh Led Zeppelin album *Presence* is released.

May 23 Robert Plant returns to the stage with Jimmy to jam with Bad Company at the LA Forum.

May 26 Led Zeppelin return to the UK. The flight back includes a humourous run-in with actor Telly Savalas.

May 27 It is heavily rumoured that the group will play a surprise show at the Marquee. Hundreds turn up but the only Zeppelin activity is a jam between John Paul Jones and The Pretty Things.

June 5 Led Zeppelin approached to play Wembley Stadium in July. They turn it down due to their involvement in completing their feature film which will be known as *The Song Remains The Same*.

June 19 Robert Plant attends the Cardiff rock festival.

July Dave Edmunds signs to Swan Song.

August Jimmy completes the mixing of their double soundtrack album at Trident. Warner co-ordinate the distribution of the film for autumn screening.

September 12 Jimmy produces an all-percussive track by John Bonham at Montreux studios. It eventually surfaces on *Coda*.

September Page is sacked by Kenneth Anger from supplying the music to his *Lucifer Rising* movie, for coming up with only 26 minutes of film music in three years.

October 5 Led Zeppelin seen in TV action when *The Old Grey Whistle Test* shows clip of 'Black Dog' from the film.

October 9 Tickets go on sale for the London screenings.

October 20 The Led Zeppelin film *The Song Remains The Same* receives its world première at Manhattan's Cinema One in New York. All the group are in attendance. All proceeds go to the Save The Children Fund. A party is held afterwards at the Pierre Hotel.

October 22 *The Song Remains The Same* soundtrack double album released worldwide. The movie receives a West Coast première in Los Angeles with a party afterwards at the Bistro.

October 23 Don Kirshner's rock concert show screens Led Zeppelin's first film clips on US TV.

October 30 Led Zeppelin announce plans to return to live action with a projected world tour kicking off in America next February.

November 2 Robert and Peter Grant interviewed by Michael Appleton on *The Old Grey Whistle Test*. 'Dazed And Confused' clip also shown.

November 4 Double European première for the film at Warner West End and ABCI Cinemas in London. All the group attend and throw a huge post première party at the Floral Hall in Covent Garden.

November 7 The film opens simultaneously in Birmingham, Glasgow, Liverpool, Cambridge, Leeds, Reading and Southampton.

November, December Group rehearsals commence in London for their 1977 touring assault. The first number they run down is 'Achilles Last Stand'.

1977

January More rehearsals at Manticore studios in Fulham. Jimmy and Robert attend The Damned's show at The Roxy in Covent Garden.

January 21 Robert and Bonzo attend the Eater, Generation X, and Damned package at the Roxy.

February 5 Announced that Zeppelin will commence their planned world tour in America at Fort Worth on February 27. Rumours abound that a festival date in the UK is being lined up for June.

February 24 US tour postponed when Robert contracts severe tonsillitis. Now due to open in Toronto in April.

March Tour dates revised again. Now opening in Dallas. UK dates now looking doubtful.

April 1 The 11th US tour opens at the Memorial Auditorium Dallas.

April 30 First leg of the tour ends with a date at the Pontiac Silverdome. In attracting 76,229, they break their own record set in Tampa in 1973, of having the largest audience for a single-act show.

May Mid-tour break. Page holidays in Cairo.

May 12 At the Ivor Novello luncheon at the Grosvenor Hotel in London, Peter Grant, Jimmy, Robert and JP accept an award for Led Zeppelin's, "Outstanding contribution to British music".

May 18 US dates resume in Birmingham, Alabama.

June 3 Rain halts a show at the Tampa stadium after 20 minutes. Due to crowd disturbances, a planned replacement date for the next day is scrapped by local authorities.

June 7-8-10-11-13-14 Six nights at Madison Square Garden, New York.

June 21-22-23-25-26-27 Six nights at the LA Forum.

June 28 Return to the UK for an 18-day break.

July Promoter Mel Bush cancels a festival due to take place at Wrotham Park on August 25, when he fails to secure Zeppelin as the headline act.

July 17 Third and final stretch of the US tour opens at the Seattle Kingdome.

July 23 After a show at the Oakland Coliseum, Peter Grant, John Bonham, tour manager Richard Cole and security man John Bindon are involved in violent clashes backstage with a member of promoter Bill Graham's staff.

July 24 The group play a very low-key second Oakland date.

July 25 The Oakland incident results in charges of battery against Grant, Bonham, Cole and Bindon. A civil suit asking £2 million in punitive damages is also filed against the group.

July 26 The group move to New Orleans for a planned show at the Superdome on July 30. Here Robert learns of the sudden death of his five-year-old-son Karac due to a stomach infection. He immediately flies back to England with Bonzo and tour manager Richard Cole. The remaining US dates are cancelled.

August 14 Page plays a charity gig with Ron Wood at the Half Moon, Plumpton.

September It is heavily rumoured that following the curtailed US tour, Led Zeppelin will split up.

September Page jams at the WEA business conference at the Metropole Hotel, Brighton with Billy Kinsley of Liverpool Express, Carl Simmons and Phil Carson.

October Jimmy Page holds a round of press interviews at the Swan Song office to dispel the split rumours.

1978

February 16 The cases against Grant, Bonham, Cole and Bindon are heard in California. All incur suspended prison sentences and fines.

May Led Zeppelin reunite at Clearwell castle in the Forest of Dean to rehearse and plan their future.

July Strongly rumoured that the group will soon return to the UK stage, possibly at Maggie Bell's Festival Hall show. Nothing materialises.

July Robert Plant sits in with various Midlands bands, including a date at the Wolverly Hall with Melvin Giganticus and The Turd Burglars.

August Plant jams with Dr Feelgood in Ibiza.

September 15 Plant, Page and Jones attend Richard Cole's wedding in Fulham.

September 16 Plant joins Dave Edmunds for the encore at Birmingham Town Hall.

October Jones and Bonham participate in Paul McCartney's Rockestra sessions at Abbey Road, London.

October Led Zeppelin commence rehearsals in London for their new album.

November 1 Plant and Jones attend the Golden Lion rock raffle in Fulham.

November 6 Led Zeppelin travel to Stockholm to record their new album at Abba's Polar Music studios.

December Initial recording completed at Polar studios. Page mixes some of the new material at his Plumpton home over Christmas.

1979

January 21 Robert Plant's wife Maureen gives birth to a son, Logan Romero.

February Mixing sessions back at Polar. Rumoured that Zeppelin will commence touring in Europe soon.

May 8 Jonesy and Robert attend Dave Edmunds' wedding reception.

May 17 Reported that Jimmy conducted the opening of Phillips Harbour in Caithness Scotland, and Robert gigged with Melvin's Marauders in Stourbridge.

May 22 Led Zeppelin announce their return to the British stage – a bill-topping show at Knebworth in August that will coincide with the release of their new album.

June 3, 4 Box offices open around the UK. Promoter Freddie Bannister reports the demand to be "the most incredible in my experience". Acts touted as possible support include Dire Straits, Fairport Convention, Joni Mitchell, Little Feat, Bob Seger, Van Morrison, The Boomtown Rats, B.B. King, Aerosmith and The Marshall Tucker Band.

June 9 Robert Plant gives his first interview in two years to Radio One's *Rock On* programme.

June 26 All the band attend the Rockpile gig at the Hammersmith Palais and after-show party at the Clarendon.

July 4 Due to exceptional demand, Led Zeppelin confirm a second Knebworth appearance on August 11.

July 4 The group hold intensive rehearsals at Bray studios.

July 19 Knebworth bill confirmed. Keith Richards and Ron Wood's New Barbarians will play during the second week.

July 19 Jimmy Page holds interviews at Swan Song in London.

July 23, 24 Led Zeppelin play two warm-up shows at the Falkoner

Theatre in Copenhagen.

July 26 Last minute line-up changes. Marshall Tucker drop out to be replaced by Commander Cody at Knebworth.

August 3 Led Zeppelin arrive at Knebworth for an evening sound-check.

August 4 First Knebworth show: Fairport Convention, Commander Cody, Chas And Dave, Southside Johnny And The Asbury Dukes, Todd Rundgren's Utopia, Led Zeppelin.

August 11 Second Knebworth show: Chas And Dave, Commander Cody, Southside Johnny And The Asbury Dukes, Todd Rundgren's Utopia, The New Barbarians, Led Zeppelin.

August 20 The new Led Zeppelin album *In Through The Out Door* released around the world.

September 17 Freddie Bannister's Tedoar company forced into liquidation following financial problems over Knebworth.

October 27 The entire Zeppelin catalogue is featured in the *Billboard* Top 200 album chart. No other group or artist in American chart history has had so many albums listed during the same week.

November 10 The Zeppelin entourage take a block booking for Abba's Wembley shows.

November 28 Plant, Jones, Bonham and Grant attend the *Melody Maker* Poll Awards reception at the Waldorf Hotel and collect a total of seven awards.

December 2 Jimmy attends the Paul McCartney, Wings gig in Brighton. Paul and Linda plus Denny Laine stay at his Plumpton home.

December 10 David Lytton Cobbold, of the Knebworth estate, fined £125 for allowing Led Zeppelin to play over their allocated time at the Knebworth shows.

December 12 Bonzo and Robert catch the Wings Birmingham show.

December 28 Tommy Vance repeats the 1969 *In Concert* Zeppelin BBC broadcast.

December 29 Robert, Jonesy and Bonzo attend the Paul McCartney and Wings Kampuchea benefit show at London's Hammersmith Odeon. Robert sings 'Little Sister' with Rockpile and all three join Paul and many others in the star-studded Rockestra finale.

1980

January 16 *The Summit*, a compilation album in aid of the International Year Of The Child, put together by K-Tel and Swan Song, is launched at a reception in London attended by Robert, Phil Lynott, Eric Clapton and others.

February 3 Robert joins Rockpile at the Birmingham Top Rank.

March 4 Bonzo travels to the Tyne Tees studio to film a live interview with Billy Connolly for the *Alright Now* TV show.

April 27 Led Zeppelin commence rehearsals at the Rainbow Theatre in London. This is in preparation for a European tour they will shortly undertake.

May 1 First tour itinerary formulated by promoter Harvey Goldsmith. Ten dates due to start in Vienna on May 22.

May 5 Rehearsals move to the New Victoria Theatre.

May 9 Tour dates revised. Now planning to open in Paris on June 16 at the Palais des Sports.

May 11 Final tour dates. It's now definitely 15 dates spanning Germany, Holland, Belgium and Austria, opening in Dortmund on June 17.

May 18 Rehearsals continue at Shepperton studios.

June 1 Reported that Jimmy is to buy Michael Caine's Windsor home for £900,000.

June 6 Completion of rehearsals at Shepperton.

June 17 Led Zeppelin open their European tour at the Westfallenhalle, Dortmund.

June 27 A show at the Messehalle in Nuremburg has to be scrapped after three numbers, due to John Bonham collapsing from physical exhaustion.

July 5 Bad Company's Simon Kirke joins the group for the encore at Munich's Olympic Halle.

July 7 Final show of the tour at the Berlin Eisport Halle.

August Holiday break for Bonzo, Robert and John Paul Jones. Jimmy moves to Windsor.

September 11 Peter Grant announces details of the Led Zeppelin: The Eighties Part One touring campaign. This will herald a return to America. Initially they will play 19 dates covering the North East and Midwest. The long term plan is to cover the South next spring. The opening date will be at the Montreal Forum on October 17.

September 18 Jimmy Page attends technical discussions at Swan Song for the upcoming tour. He inspects a model set-up of the stage rig they plan to use for the Led Zeppelin: The Eighties Part One campaign.

September 21 Massive ticket demand reported in America.

September 24 John Bonham leaves Worcestershire to meet up with the rest of the group at Bray studios for the first rehearsal for the upcoming US tour. After the rehearsal the entourage return to Page's Windsor home. Bonzo falls asleep after a heavy drinking session.

September 25 At around 1.45 pm, Zeppelin sound technician Benji Le Fevre checks Bonzo's room to see why he hasn't stirred. After checking his pulse he immediately calls a doctor. Shortly after, John Bonham is pronounced dead, having inhaled his own vomit. By 7 pm, the news has leaked to the press and is carried as a major news item on every TV and radio station in the country. At the same time, as yet unaware of the tragedy, over 1,000 fans in Chicago are queuing for early copies of the Chicago Tribune which carries mail order ticket details of Led Zeppelin's four planned concerts at the Chicago Stadium in November.

September 26 In the wake of the tragedy, Thames Valley Police announce there are no suspicious circumstances involved.

September 27 Tributes pour in from across the world. The US tour is cancelled and speculation is rife that Zeppelin will now disband.

October 7 Following an inquest, a

verdict of accidental death is returned on John Bonham.

October 10 John Bonham's funeral held at Rushock, Worcestershire .

October 18 Rumours abound that Cozy Powell, Aynsley Dunbar, Peter Criss, Paul Thompson and Carmine Appice will be named as a replacement for Bonzo.

November 7 The remaining members of Led Zeppelin travel to Jersey to discuss their future. On their return, they hold a meeting with Peter Grant at the Savoy Hotel in London to announce their intention to retire Led Zeppelin as a group.

December 4 Led Zeppelin issue the following press statement: "We wish it to be known that the loss of our dear friend, and the deep respect we have for his family, together with the sense of undivided harmony felt by ourselves and our manager, have led us to decide that we could not continue as we were."

Track Index